CRITICS PRAISE

Black Man's Burden:

"Killens' aggressiveness typifies the new direction which the civil rights movement is taking. For Killens, with his finger pointed squarely at our white faces, is not alone.... We may not like all that we hear, but if we fail to listen, we do so at our peril." —*The Kansas City Star*

"...a passionate and uninhibited book, entirely honest, by a writer who is wholeheartedly committed to the racial struggle." —*The Oregon Journal*

"...a forceful book, written by a man who loves his country and who believes that the future of the American Negro is in America." —*Bestsellers Magazine*

"...a stunning writer...a vigorous book."
 —*The World Telegram and The Sun*

"...an important book containing power, irony, humor, candor and truth." —*The Dayton News*

John Oliver Killens has been called "the most gifted American novelist living."* His first novel, *Youngblood*, was hailed as "an astonishing performance."** His reputation was secured with the publication in 1963 of *And Then We Heard the Thunder*, a close contender for a Pulitzer Prize.

**The San Francisco People's Worl*
***The Saturday Review Syndicate*

BLACK MAN'S BURDEN
was originally published by Trident Press.

*Are there paperbound books you want
but cannot find in your retail stores?*

You can get any title in print in:
Pocket Book editions • Pocket *Cardinal* editions • Permabook editions or Washington Square Press editions. Simply send retail price, local sales tax, if any, plus 15¢ to cover mailing and handling costs for each book wanted to:

MAIL SERVICE DEPARTMENT
POCKET BOOKS • A Division of Simon & Schuster, Inc.
1 West 39th Street • New York, New York 10018
Please send check or money order. We cannot be responsible for cash.
Catalogue sent free on request.

Titles in these series are also available at discounts in quantity lots for industrial or sales-promotional use. For details write our Special Projects Agency: The Benjamin Company, Inc., 485 Madison Avenue, New York, N.Y. 10022.

Freeman

Black Man's Burden

John Oliver Killens

PUBLISHED BY POCKET BOOKS NEW YORK

BLACK MAN'S BURDEN

Trident Press edition published July, 1965

A Pocket Book edition
1st printing .... April, 1969

This *Pocket Book* edition includes every word
contained in the original, higher-priced edition. It is printed
from brand-new plates made from completely reset, clear, easy-to-read
type. *Pocket Book* editions are published by Pocket Books, a division
of Simon & Schuster, Inc., 630 Fifth Avenue, New York, N.Y. 10020.
Trademarks registered in the United States and other countries.

Standard Book Number: 671-75360-6.
Library of Congress Catalog Card Number: 65-24155.
Copyright, ©, 1965, by John Oliver Killens. All rights reserved.
Printed in the U.S.A.

FOR

my Father

CONTENTS

1

The Black Psyche

WHEN I WAS A BOY in Macon, Georgia, one of the greatest compliments a benevolent white man could give a Negro was usually found in the obituary column of the local newspaper: "He was a black man, but he had a white heart." And the burden of every black man was supposedly just a little easier to bear that day. It was a time when many of us black folk laughed at the antics of *Amos 'n' Andy* and wept copious tears at a ridiculous movie very aptly titled *Imitation of Life*. Most of us looked at life through the eyes of white America.

The great fictional (and film) masterpieces on the American racial theme usually fell into two categories. One theme dealt with the utter heart-break of the mulatto, who rejected his black blood and was in turn rejected by his white blood. A variation of this theme was the shattering experience of "passing." The other theme was the "Uncle Tom," or what I prefer to call the "Gunga Din," theme. This one also had many variations, but over all there was the image created by that great apologist for colonialism, Rudyard Kipling, of a man who

> *. . . For all 'is dirty 'ide*
> *'E was white, clear white, inside*
> *When 'e went to tend the wounded*
> *   under fire!*

With some "additional touches" by Hollywood, dear old "white inside" Gunga evolved as a marvelous figment of Western man's wistful imagination, the personification of his wish fulfillment. Remember Gunga? He was a water boy for the British regiment and in the movie version, finally blew the bugle against his own people. And how "white" inside could a "noble savage" be?

I am waging a quiet little campaign at the moment to substitute the term "Gunga Din" for that much maligned character "Uncle Tom" in designating the contemporary water boys who still blow the bugles for old Massa. For although Mrs. Stowe's beloved "Uncle Tom" was indeed an Uncle Tom, as we understand the term today, he nevertheless, in the final confrontation, chose death rather than blow the whistle on his people.

Variations of the Gunga Din theme were seen in a rash of movie epics, like *Gone with the Wind* and *Virginia* and *Kentucky,* etc., *ad infinitum, ad nauseam,* always played magnificently with tongue in cheek by such stalwarts as Hattie McDaniel and Louise Beavers. In the great emotional scene the black "mammy" was usually in the big house, weeping and moaning over little pure-white-as-the-driven-snow Missy Anne, who had just sneezed, while Mammy's own young-un was dying of double pneumonia, unattended, down in the cabins. All in all, the slaves were presented as carefree and contented in their idyllic degradation. If the black man really believed in this romantic version of American slavery, he would have long since wasted away, pining for those good old happy-go-lucky days of bondage.

Last year I did considerable research on that bygone "utopian" era, and I got a very different picture, slightly less romantic. I found that the slaves were so happy that most of the plantation owners couldn't afford the astronomical rates of fire insurance. Those rapturous slaves kept setting fire to the cotton patches, burning down the plantation, every day the good Lord sent them. They organized countless insurrections, killed their masters, poisoned their mistresses, even put spiders in the Big House soup. They demonstrated their contentment in most peculiar ways.

The point is, most white Americans cling desperately to these wish-fulfillment fantasies, but most of us Negroes have become unbelievers. We don't break into cheers any more when the cowboys chase the Indians across the movie screen, or when the Army finally captures old John Brown. Indeed, our favorite epic of the west has become Custer's Last Stand. Sitting Bull is a colored hero. Many black folk wish that this mighty warrior had been an American Negro.

I shall never forget an evening I spent in a movie house in Hollywood watching the closed-circuit television broadcast of the first Patterson-Johannson fight, and the great shame I felt for my white countrymen that night as they began to sense a possible victory for the white foreigner over the black American. Forgotten entirely was the fact that softhearted Floyd Patterson was a fellow countryman. Color superseded patriotism.

As I sat there hearing shouted exhortations, like "Kill the nigger!", I felt that Patterson and I were aliens in a strange and hostile country, and that Ingemar was at home among his people. In fairness to my countrymen in the closed circuits of America that night, their reactions were not intellectual, not even willful. They were spontaneous, not unlike a conditioned reflex. This ecstasy at the sudden emergence of a new white hope came from their hearts, their souls, their bellies. It was their white insides reacting.

I have been told that this incident had no racial implications at all, that these rabid Johannson fans were merely upholding the old American tradition of rooting for the underdog. Well, I was also rooting for the underdog, and I knew that, win or lose, the underdog in America was Floyd Patterson, Harry Belafonte, Emmett Till, Rosa Parks, Meredith, Poitier, the black American, I, *me*. The words "Kill the nigger!" could not possibly have come screaming from my throat, subconsciously, unconsciously, or otherwise. Nor could they from any other black man's throat.

Just as surely as East is East and West is West, there is a "black" psyche in America and there is a "white" one, and the sooner we face up to this psychological, social, and cultural reality, the sooner the twain shall meet. Our emotional chemistry is different from white America's. Your joy is very often our anger, and your despair our hope. Most of us came here in chains, and many of you came here to escape your chains. Your freedom was our slavery, and therein lies the bitter difference in the way we look at life. You created the myth of the faithful slave, but we know that the "loyal slave" is a contradiction in terms. We understand, though, that the master must always make himself believe in the undying love of his slave.

Ironically enough, the fathers of our magnificent Revolution, Washington and Jefferson, themselves owned hundreds of human chattels, and even though the great Thomas Jefferson made many speeches against the peculiar institution, he was never able to convince himself to the extent of manumitting his own slaves during his lifetime. Surely the great irony of the situation did not escape my ancestors back in the days of the Revolution. And now, today, it does not escape their great-great-grandchildren. When we hear some white statesman use the phrase "the Free World," even though the same white statesman may very well be the Governor of the State of Mississippi or Alabama, or even President of these United States, for that matter, we—as the slaves of Washington and Jefferson must have done—stare at him incredulously and cannot believe our ears. And we wonder how this word "freedom" can have such vastly different meanings, such conflicting connotations.

But the time has come for you (white America) and me (black America) to work this thing out once and for all, to examine and evaluate the differences between us and the differences inside us. Time is swiftly running out, and a new dialogue is indispensable. It is so long overdue it is already half past midnight.

And let us be clear on one thing. My fight is not to be a white man in a black skin, but to inject some black blood, some black intelligence, some black humaneness, into the pallid mainstream of American life—culturally, socially, psychologically, philosophically. This is the truer, deeper meaning of the Negro revolt which is not yet a revolution—to get America ready for the middle of the twentieth century, which is already magnificently here.

This new epoch has caught our country (yours and mine) dozing in a sweet nostalgia of the good old days. Our country slumbers in a world of yesteryears, before Africa and Asia got up off their knees and threw off the black man's burden. The good old days when you threw pennies to the "natives." And there were gunboats in the China Sea and Big Stick policies and Monroe Doctrines and "Gold Coasters" from the U.K. sipped their gin-and-tonics in Accra and Lagos and talked about the "natives," as they basked in their roles of Great White Fathers in that best of all possible worlds.

That world is gone forever, and black and brown men everywhere are glad, deep in their hearts, though most Western men are chagrined, which may be the understatement of the century. The title of the great Duke Ellington's song has come true: "Things Ain't What They Used to Be." And the good news, or the bad news, depending on your point of view, is: Things ain't never going to be anything like they used to be. This is why the world is becoming too much for Western men, however liberal, even some radical Western men, whoever you are, and wherever. But the world is becoming more and more to my liking, to my taste and in my image. It gladdens my heart to see black and brown men and women walk with dignity in the United Nations, in affirmation of the manhood and the selfhood of the entire human race.

The American Negro, you see, is an Anglo-Saxon invention, a role the Anglo-Saxon gentleman created for the black man in this drama known euphemistically as the American Way of Life. It began as an economic expedient, frankly, because you wanted somebody to work for nothing. It is still that, but now it is much more than that. It has become a way of life within a way of life, socially, economically, psychologically, philosophically. The Negro Invention, hatched in the brave New World, ultimately and rapidly became a rationalization for the colonializing of three-quarters of the earth's peoples. All non-whites throughout the world became "niggers" and therefore proper material for "civilizing" and "Christianizing" (cruel euphemisms for colonization, exploitation, genocide, and slavery).

And now, in the middle of the twentieth century, I, the Negro, like my counterparts in Asia and Africa and South America and on the islands of the many seas, am refusing to be your "nigger" any longer. Even some of us "favored," "talented," "unusual," ones are refusing to be your educated, sophisticated, split-leveled "niggers" any more. We refuse to look at ourselves through the eyes of white America.

We are not fighting for the right to be like you. We respect ourselves too much for that. When we advocate freedom, we mean freedom for us to be black, or brown, and you to be white and yet live together in a free and equal society. This is the only way that integration can bring dignity for both of us. I, for one, am growing weary of those well-meaning white liberals who are forever telling me they don't know what color I am. The very fact that they always single me out at every cocktail party to gratuitously make me the beneficiary of their blessed assurances gives the lie to their pronouncements.

My fight is not for racial sameness but for racial equality and against racial prejudice and discrimination. I work for the day when black people will be free of the racist pressures to be white like you; a day when "good hair" and "high yaller" and bleaching cream and hair straighteners will be obsolete. What a tiresome place America would be if freedom meant we all had to think alike or be the same color or wear that same gray flannel suit! That road leads to the conformity of the graveyard.

If relationships are to improve between us Americans, black and white and otherwise, if the country is to be changed and saved, we will have to face up to the fact that differences do exist between us. All men react to life through man-made symbols. Even our symbolic reactions are different from yours. To give a few examples:

In the center of a little Southern town near the border of Mississippi there is a water tower atop which sits a large white cross, illumined at night with a lovely (awesome to Negroes) neon brightness, which can be seen for miles. To most white Americans, seeing it for the first time, it is a beacon that symbolizes the Cross upon which Jesus died, and it gives them a warm feeling. But it puts an angry knot in a black man's belly. To him it symbolizes the very "Christian" K.K.K. Just as to the average white man, a courthouse, even in Mississippi, is a place where justice is dispensed. Yet to me, the black man, it is a place where justice is dispensed with.

We even have a different historical perspective. Most white Americans, even today, look upon the Reconstruction period as a horrible time of "carpetbagging," and "black politicians," and "black corruption," the absolutely lowest ebb in the Great American Story. Oh, the oceans of bitter tears American writers have wept for that ill-begotten era. Oh, the shame of it all, the way those Southern patriots were treated after that unfortunate war, that horrendous misunderstanding.

We black folk, however, look upon Reconstruction as the most democratic period in the history of this nation; a time when the dream the founders dreamed was almost within reach and right there for the taking; a time of democratic fervor the like of which was never seen before and never since. For all we know, it was a time when America could have won the world but lost it, probably forever. We don't share your feeling that the Negro was not ready for the franchise. We think that the first slaves on that first slave ship were men and women and therefore capable of being citizens anywhere. This is our understanding of democracy. We are not impressed with the mess white Americans (educated and illiterate ones) have made of this Republic, and apparently, because of their whiteness, they were born ready. Apparently, they were endowed by "their creator."

For us, Reconstruction was the time when two black men were Senators in the Congress of the United States from the State of Mississippi; when black men served in the legislatures of all the states in Dixie; and when those "corrupt" legislatures gave to the South its first public-school education. And the lowest ebb for us black folk came on the heels of the Great Betrayal, when the government in Washington turned us over to the benevolent Ku Klux Klan and the Knights of the Camellias.

Nor do we share your romantic view of Rob Lee and Jeff Davis. Certainly, to most of us who have thought about the matter, they were traitors, pure and simple. We put them in the same inglorious category as the infamous Benedict Arnold.

I shall never forget the feeling I had one morning in the fall of 1957, in a Hollywood hotel, when I awoke and tuned into the outside world of television. There before my eyes were American soldiers, black and white, rolling into Little Rock, Arkansas, with their rifles at the ready. I cried that morning. I unashamedly wept. Wept for the moment that had been so long in the coming, the moment when for the first time in my life I felt that the nation gave a damn about *me*. One courageous black woman and eight innocent beautiful black children had laid down the gauntlet and brought the nation to the brink of human decency.

Whatever the political considerations that dictated the move, I felt that the nation had committed itself again, in a way it had not done since Reconstruction. When I saw the Star-Spangled Banners waving from those jeeps and tanks as they rolled endlessly into Little Rock that morning, Old Glory meant more to me, the black American, *me,* than ever before in my life's brief span, including the forty-one months I spent in the service of my country during World War II. Oh yes, we black folk find it difficult to understand the nation's hesitation about sending troops to Mississippi to guarantee free elections when we read of American boys dying thousands of miles from home to ensure freedom for the Vietnamese. The subtlety escapes us.

Even our white hero symbols are different from yours. You give us moody Abe Lincoln, but many of us prefer John Brown, whom most of you hold in contempt as a fanatic; meaning, of course, that the firm dedication of any white man to the freedom of the black man is *prima-facie* evidence of perversion or insanity.

You look upon these times as the Atomic Age, the Space Age, the Cold War Era. But I believe that when the history of our times is written, it will not be so important who reached the moon first or who made the largest bomb. I believe the great significance will be that this was the century when most of mankind achieved freedom and human dignity, the age when racial prejudices became obsolete. For me, this is the Freedom Century.

So now it is time for you to understand us, because it is becoming increasingly hazardous for you not to. Dangerous for both of us. As Richard Wright said in his *Twelve Million Black Voices,* voices you chose not to heed: "Each day when you see us black folk upon the dusty land of your farms or upon the hard pavement of your city streets, you usually take us for granted and think you know us, but our history is far stranger than you suspect, and we are not what we seem." The Rev. Ralph Abernathy of Montgomery put it more humorously when he said that the new Negro of Montgomery had stopped laughing when he wasn't tickled and scratching when he didn't itch.

At the turn of the century, Negro prophet William Edward Burghardt DuBois warned the Western world: "The problem of the twentieth century is the problem of the color line." But who listens to a black prophet at such a time of endless frontiers for the white pioneers and missionaries? Now, in the middle of that same century, we are bringing down the curtain on this role you cast us in, and we will no longer be a party to our own degradation. We have become unbelievers, no longer believing in the absolute superiority of the white man's juju. You have never practiced what you preached. Why should we believe in you? Why would we want to be like you?

Yes, we are different from you and we are not invisible men, Ralph Ellison notwithstanding. We are the most visible of Americans.

Last spring, Charles Harris, Negro editor for Doubleday, and I had drinks at the Playboy Club in New York. We were so visible, everybody who came into the place stared at us more than they did the semi-naked bunnies. "Who're they? Ralph Bunche and Sonny Liston, or Joe Louis and Sammy Davis, Junior? Or maybe Willie Mays and Martin Luther King?" Oh yes, we have a very high degree of visibility.

But white Americans are great pretenders. Millions of you wish we were invisible, and so you make believe we are. You'd like to wish us out of existence so that the whole world would not see us, because our very life in this country, as black people, gives the lie before the world to your protestations of freedom and human brotherhood. The white man's juju is powerful stuff, but it cannot wish the Negro into invisibility. So you try the next best thing, pretending you can't tell one of us from the other.

The point is: Since we no longer look at ourselves through *your* eyes, our visibility, to *your* eyes, is a total irrelevance, to *us*. We no longer look to you for our identity. But this self-delusion on *your* part (that you don't see us and that you can't tell us one from the other) is dangerous for you and for *our* country. You always knew the difference between the "field" slave and the "house" one; between the "bad nigger" and the "good" one; between Gunga Din and old Nat Turner, between Dubois and Booker Washington.

In the summer and fall of 1961 I traveled in a Land Rover 12,000 miles through Africa. I talked to people in the cities, on the farms, in the villages. I talked with workers, farmers, artists, market women, ministers of state, politicians, teachers, and the same question was asked me everywhere I went: "How can we believe your country's professions of good will to us, with whom they have not lived, when they deny human dignity to you who come from us and have lived with them for centuries and helped to build their great civilization?"

It is a question that America has to answer to the entire New World of Africa and Asia. The only way we Americans, black and white, can answer it affirmatively is to make freedom and democracy work at home, here and now. Most Negroes still believe that the ultimate solution for us is in America, and I am as firmly convinced that the ultimate salvation of America is in the Negro.

The Negro loves America enough to criticize her fundamentally. Most white Americans simply can't be bothered. Ironically enough, in the middle of the twentieth century, the Negro is the new white hope. To live castrated in a great white harem and yet somehow maintain our black manhood and humanity—this is the essence of the new man created out of the Negro Invention. History may render the verdict that this was the greatest legacy handed to the New World by the West.

There are glaring exceptions to every rule, but it is a truism that American Negroes are the only people in America who, as a people, are for change. This is true, again, not innately because of our color, but because of what America made of our color. The *status quo* has ever been the bane of black existence.

We black folk have learned many lessons during our sojourn in this place. One of them is the truth of the Ghana proverb, "Only a fool points to his origin with his left hand." We are becoming prouder and prouder of our origins. And we know the profound difference between pride and arrogance; the difference, if you will, between James Meredith and Ross Barnett, both of Mississippi. Our dialogue will not be protest but affirmation of the human dignity of all people everywhere. Yes, our aim is to create a dialogue in full vindication of every lonesome disinherited "nigger," every black and brown man born of woman who ever dwelt upon this alien earth, which means, of course, that all mankind would be vindicated regardless of race, color, or religion. Our dialogue is anti-racist.

Sure, I know that there are white folk who want America to be the land of the free and home of the brave, but there are far too few of them, and many of them are rarely brave. I cherish old John Brown and Garrison and William Moore and Mike Schwerner and Andy Goodman and all the other winter soldiers. Let the winter patriots increase their ranks. Let those who truly love America join the valiant Negro Revolt and change and save our country.

2

**The Black Writer
Vis-à-Vis
His Country**

I BELIEVE IT WAS George Bernard Shaw who once said that America was the first country in history to move from barbarism to decadence without going through civilization. I construe the statement of this estimable British gentleman of letters to mean that our country has been in such a hurry becoming the wealthiest and the most powerful nation in the world, it has hardly had the time

or stomach for the niceties of culture and civilization. Indeed, it has been in such unseemly haste,
it has not even taken the time to bring into reality
some of the most magnificent literature ever written about the rights of men. I refer, of course,
to the Bill of Rights, the Declaration of Independence, and the Constitution of the United
States.

So a cultural revolution is desperately needed,
here and now, to un-brainwash the entire American people, black and white. For the people of
this land have been the victims of a mighty brain-
wash that has continued unabated for the last four
hundred years. Perhaps Negro artists must assume
an uneven load in this cultural revolution because,
as black folk, they know America better than she
knows herself. The laws of survival dictate that
the slave must know the many turns and twists
and quirks of his master. Moreover, the Negro
remembers better than anybody else the American dream, deferred and forgotten by most Americans. He remembers, because he lives constantly
the dream's negation, yet lives for the day when
the dream will become a reality. He could never
take for granted the Declaration of Independence,
the Bill of Rights, the Constitution of these United
States. He could never become blasé about
the dream. In a word, your humble servant, the
black American, has borne the brunt of the mil-

lions of little white lies America has told the world about herself and about the Negro.

Since the so-called American Indian is practically extinct, it is highly probable that the only indigenous American culture is that of the American Negro. The Negro was invented in America. Only in America. In the main, his has been a culture of revolt, of protest and revolution; a culture that is expressed very clearly in the Negro spirituals. More often than not, they are still interpreted as songs of a happy, childlike people, satisfied with their lot in this world and looking forward to the Hereafter, where the streets would be paved with gold and overflow with milk and honey. Why do Americans still hang on in desperation to the image of the happy and contented slave? "DIDN'T MY LORD DELIVER DANIEL? WHY NOT EVERY MAN?" is not exactly a happy and contented lyric!

From all sides pressure is put upon the Negro artist to deny his culture, his roots, his selfhood. How many black writers have you heard engage in this abject self-denial: "I am not a Negro writer. I am a writer who happens to be a Negro." But the truth of the matter is that we black Americans are all Negroes (African-Americans, if you prefer) who happen to have become writers, painters, lawyers, subway motormen, doctors, teachers, ditchdiggers, pickpockets, hustlers, or whatever. We see life from the vantage point of being Negro. A creative writer writes out of his particular frame of reference, which is the sum total of his life's experience, and he had better come to terms with it as hurriedly as possible.

Yet from Hollywood to Broadway to Madison Avenue, I hear variations of the same refrain: "John, why do you insist upon writing about Negroes? Why don't you write about people?" As often as I've heard that one, it never fails to jar me, laboring, as I always have, under the illusion that Negroes *are* people. Another goes like this: "The thing I liked about your story, John, it was universal. It could have been about anybody."

Well—I submit that a story that could have been about anybody is probably about precisely nobody at all. Negroes are the only people in this world who are set apart because of who they are, and at the same time told to forget who they are by the same people who set them apart in the first place.

Now, then, how could I, John Killens, write a valid story about a Chinese peasant in the hinterlands of China? No matter how *universal* my literary approach, I would never be able to get close to the Chinese peasant's specifics, the cultural and the idiomatic meanings of his life, the unique Chineseness of him, which are his and only his. Besides, I could never muster up that much racial arrogance.

I am convinced that when Western man speaks of universality, he is referring to an Anglo-Saxon universality, which includes a very meager sector of this young and aging universe. Every line of Sean O'Casey's works exudes a sense of Irishness. Dostoevski bared the Russian soul. No critic ever questioned their universality. But to write out of the frame of reference of an American Negro is *ipso facto* anti-universal.

Herbert Hill, newly blossoming literary expert on Negro affairs, in his introduction to *Soon One Morning,* an anthology of "New Writing by American Negroes," acclaimed Ralph Ellison for all the wrong reasons, because Ellison's work, according to Hill, "transcends the traditional preoccupations of the Negro writer. . . . Today the Negro artist, as he enters into the mainstream of contemporary literature, feels a new strength and refuses to be limited to racial protest. . . . As the Negro writer moves beyond his anger, he develops a new concern for literary discipline and control. . . ."

Well, Mr. Hill, the American mainstream contains some rather sickly fish; if Ellison did indeed enter the "mainstream," the mainstream got more than it gave. It is a pretty puny achievement to join the mainstream, and a puny achievement is precisely what Ellison's novel was not.

The mainstream is jammed with writers like Updike and Salinger, who write page after page of precious prose about absolutely nothing. With the whole Western world as their potential canvas, and swiftly going to pot and trying desperately to take the rest of civilization with it, such writers flee in panic because the New World is becoming too much for them. They escape into minutiae of tight little islands of personal insignificance and Oedipus complexes. The American mainstream has come up with a crop of literary nitpickers, most of them entirely without testicles. So now they want to castrate the Negro writer, too. Is this the stream Herb Hill would lead black writers into?

But the motley crew of little white fathers are saying nothing new. They merely repeat the old refrains pontifically, as if they're saying something startling and fresh. You say to yourself, I've heard that song before, for underneath there is always this veiled admonition to black writers: "You'll never win the prizes or the critics' adulation unless you cool your anger and lay that pistol down. Keep criticizing society and you'll continue to incur the wrath of us white reviewers, who are not bad fellows at all and would really like to bring you into the fold. Oh yes, in spite of the fact that you are a Negro, you too can join the club if you'll just play down your Negro-ness."

But a writer who writes to get into the mainstream and win National Book Awards and plaudits from the critics is in trouble with his muse. A creative writer is not a statesman. He must tell as much of the truth as he knows the painful truth to be, and let the flak fall where it may. Writing is a hazardous pursuit. The flak might very well fall back on the writer and put a large hole in his head. It has something to do with the law of gravity. What goes up must come down. Artists are forever at war with society, and if the artist is a black man in the Free World he is doubly at war and the war's consequences are especially dangerous for him. But he must fight in any event, for the consequences of his temporizing are fraught with even greater danger.

When Ernest Hemingway was interviewed by the *Paris Review* a few years before he died and asked what kind of advice he would give young writers, he answered that a writer needed two things—a sense of justice and a built-in, shockproof shit detector. Obviously a writer also needs artistic talent, but granting his talent, he desperately needs these two attributes Mr. Hemingway so graphically described.

As a writer, I must believe with all my mind

and heart and soul in the ancient adage "You shall know the truth and the truth shall set you free." In a far deeper sense even than men of the cloth, writers must be searchers for the truth; men and women whose life's mission is to explore the truth of man's relationship to man. And I, for one, believe the basic truth of what my grandmother used to say. "Aah Lord, honey, the half ain't never been told." There is nothing in the world that I believe more than the wisdom of that statement. If I believed, as some Western men continually assert, that everything has already been said and it's just a question now of how differently you say it, that all is semantics from now on, I would put the cover on my typewriter and never uncover it again. As a writer, I must believe that most of what has already been said is a pack of lies, or, in some instances, mistakes, to be more charitable to makers of the myths. It is up to the writer to create a new vision for mankind. He must be forever asking questions. He must ask the unaskable. Was "Plato's Republic" a Republic? Was Jefferson democrat or slaveholder? This world can't possibly be man's best effort, or we're all doomed to destruction or the madhouse. Life must make more sense than it has up to this point.

Did Shakespeare's "Macbeth" utter an everlasting truth? Have all our yesteryears lighted fools the way to dusty death? "Out, out, brief candle!" Macbeth shouts. "Life's but a walking shadow; a poor player, that struts and frets his hour upon the stage, and then is heard no more: it is a tale told by an idiot, full of sound and fury, signifying nothing." Or did Langston Hughes come closer to *our* truth when he asked: "What happens to a dream too long deferred?"

I am a writer, first of all, and precisely because the world stinks and I want to change it. Yes, I mean it, and any writer worth his salt is up to the same subversive business. This is the way things always were, the eternal confrontation between the artist and society. Every time I sit down to the typewriter, with every line I put on paper, I am out to change the world, to capture reality, to melt it down and forge it into something entirely different. The portrait of the artist as a human being is one of profound frustration, because although he knows that "change" is one of the inevitable laws of the universe in the context of time and space, change in human nature is imperceptible. That is why the French have a saying: "The more things change the more they remain the same." But the earth *does* move. And things *do* change.

Since everybody "knows" the artist is the maladjusted one, I plead guilty to the charge. To be perfectly adjusted in a crazy, impractical, unreasonable society hellbent for its own annihilation seems tantamount to remaining blissful in a raging booby hatch. This is what drove Van Gogh to suicide. He was naïve enough to want to make sense in a crazy world. His sin was that he took life seriously and he loved mankind. *Ergo,* he was an idiot before his peers. He wanted to make sense out of a senseless society, and therefore he was a damn fool. But what is the verdict a century after he departed? Whom does the world remember, Van Gogh or his contemporaries?

But despite the current Negro Revolt, which is not yet a revolution, rumors to the contrary, the American Negro remains a cultural nonentity as far as books, television, movies, and Broadway are concerned. It is as if twenty million Americans did not exist; as if twenty million people were committed to oblivion. A Negro child can read at home or go to school and look into his school books, come home and watch television or maybe go to an occasional movie, and follow this routine from day to day, month to month, year to year, and hardly, if ever, see a reflection of himself in the mass-communications media. This has a tremendously negative impact on a child, who must have a sense of belonging and not of being here by toleration. A child must have a sense of selfhood, a knowledge that he is not here by sufferance, that his forebears contributed to the country and to the world down through the years.

America knows that the blood, sweat, tears, and muscles of black folk helped to build this mighty country. You wouldn't be so high and mighty if it weren't for me. You built this country on the black backs of my forefathers. Slave labor, that's what it really was, slave labor at a time when slavery was already obsolete throughout much of the earth. That's how you constructed your great temples and stored them with riches. That's how you got so far ahead of the rest of man in treasures stored up here on earth. You cruelly exploited my forebears. And now you deny my children a cultural existence. You pretend they are invisible.

I know the impact. I was a black boy once in Georgia. I remember. And I know the impact now, because I am the father of two African-Americans in New York City. I remember when my son was nine or ten years old, my great friend Langston Hughes came to dinner and brought my son a book he had written called *Famous American Negroes*. In it Langston had written, for children, stories about the Negro heroes of American history. Of Harriet Tubman, Frederick Douglass, Crispus Attucks, and Benjamin Banneker. This book opened many doors for my son, Chuck. He was so thrilled he took it to school the next day and showed it to the teacher, then asked, demanded really, that she read it to the class.

We lived at the time in the now "infamous" Bedford-Stuyvesant area in Brooklyn and the school was about fifty-fifty in its composition (meaning Negro-white, not co-educational). This was just before the great white exodus from the community had developed into full-scale, panic-stricken, disorderly retreat. The teacher read passages of the book to my son's class and that night at the dinner table I asked him how it had gone.

"It was wonderful, Daddy! Everybody enjoyed the book." Then Chuck frowned and said, "But you know, Daddy, nobody at that school knows anything about Negro culture or Negro history."

"I suppose it's understandable that the white children don't know," I said.

"Oh no, Daddy, I mean the Negro children, too. Not even the teacher knows." And then he poked out his chest and said very proudly, "I'm the only one in that school that knows *anything* about Negro history or culture."

I looked at him and wanted to laugh and shout for the joy and pride he felt. At the same time I wanted to cry for all the black kids all over America caught up in what playwright Ted Ward has called the Big White Fog, never knowing that they have ever been anything and therefore never believing they'll ever amount to anything.

My daughter, Barbara, was then six years old. We lived in a brownstone on Lafayette Avenue, the parlor floor and basement. She would sit in the living room on the parlor floor and stare at the idiot box for hour upon hour. What program didn't matter, she even watched the commercials. We figured this was rather precocious for one of her tender age, for some of the commercials were better than the programs. Ultimately the fog lifted (for us, I mean), and we realized that our daughter was watching to see herself reflected on the television screen, a black man or woman presented with dignity, for she already knew the difference between dignity and *Amos 'n' Andy*. When once or twice during a long and arduous vigil she saw a black face on the white screen, she would run downstairs where we usually were, shouting, "Daddy! Mommy! Negro on TV!" But by the time we got upstairs he or she would be gone.

When we first moved to the neighborhood where we now live, Barbara was the only Negro in her class. She came home from school one day in tears. The history teacher had told the class that the Civil War was fought too soon, that the slaves weren't ready for freedom, and were happy and contented on the old plantation. Barbara took on the entire class and the teacher. "I don't know if I said the right things, Daddy. But I knew that what that teacher was saying didn't sound like anything I'd heard at home."

She burst into tears again as if her heart would surely break. Barbara was a happy girl most of the time. She rarely cried. She ran headlong into life, smiling, laughing, tripping, falling, getting up and running smack dab into life again, with hardly ever a thought about the very high cost of living. How could a teacher be so vicious to such a tenderhearted child? Or was the lady just plain ignorant?

I know a young black artist whose art is a monument to black life in America. He renders a toast to life in every stroke of his talented brush. Yet when I saw Tom Feelings at a meeting a few months ago, he was disheartened and told me he was leaving America. He had been going to the public schools of Bedford-Stuyvesant and giving chalk talks to black children on Negro and African history. But he explained that he could no longer do so because he realized more and more that the Negro kids thought themselves ugly. Because they were black. He said it was just too much for him. He thought they were beautiful; they thought they were ugly. Obviously their parents agreed with them. How else can one interpret stocking caps and straightening combs and bleaching cream?

"John, I've got to get to Africa. I've got to go to a place where black children know who they are and what they are and know that they're beautiful and that they are somebody. I've got to go some damn place where black folk don't think of themselves as 'niggers.' "

He was almost in tears. I knew the desperate feeling. From generation to generation the "nigger" feeling is handed down from parent to child. The feeling that what is white is right, and what is black is wrong. White is the symbol of purity and virginity and everything else that is good and powerful and eternal. Oh, how many times in the days of my youth did I sit in the humble pews of black churches and hear the wonderful, soulful, beautiful, hard-working black sisters, young and old, shout supplications of utter futility: "Wash me, Heavenly Father, And I will be as white as snow!"

The Western world deliberately made black the symbol of all that was evil and ugly. Black Friday, blacklist, Black Plague, black look, blackmail. Oh, the way the white Establishment made us hate ourselves. "A nigger ain't shit!" is a black password, a common utterance of black folks. You took a great people from a great continent and turned them into "niggers." That is the job you accomplished in the name of "civilizing the natives" and "Christianizing the pagans." That is the essence of what America is, from the black man's point of view. The land of the "niggermakers."

This distorted image of the Negro has its negative effect on your children too. It gives them a distorted picture of this earth and of human potential and ill-equips them to live in a world, three-quarters of which is colored and fast becoming free and independent.

That is why my friends from the African embassies run into difficulties "Down South" in Atlanta and New Orleans and even "Up South" in New York City. To the average American, they are simply "niggers." In a way, I cannot truthfully say that I am sorry. As long as indignities are commonplace for black Americans, it is all to the good for black brothers from across the seas to labor under no illusions as to the (universal) American attitude toward men and women of color. I am not sadistic. Neither am I masochistic. I just don't want America to hoodwink black folk throughout the world. Let us set things straight at home first.

Along with the fight to desegregate the schools, we must desegregate the entire cultural statement of America; we must desegregate the minds of the American people. If we merely succeed in desegregating the school buildings, we may very well find that we have won the battle and lost the war. Integration begins the day after the minds of the American people are desegregated. This is the great challenge to all American writers, but especially to the black writer. Who will tell the real story of America if the black writer doesn't? Certainly not the gentlemen of the "mainstream" who still believe in Gunga Din and Uncle Tom and Aunt Jemima, or the "avant-garde," the rebels who are really anti-revolutionary. Jean Genêt and his genre, the "theater of the absurd," the "beatnik," the "new wave," would appear to be merely Johnny-come-lately Kiplings. Apologists for white supremacy die hard and recur in varying disguises.

Behind the "avant-garde's" beards and dark glasses, they rationalize, apologize, as they strut and posture. The underlying statements of *The Blacks* and *The Balcony* are the same, that all civilization stinks, *period*. "When the *have-nots* overthrow the *haves,* nothing will really change except the relative positions of the adversaries. It will be the same thing all over again. There is no revolution ever. It's the same merry-go-round, so stop the world, I want to get off." Well, pardon me, fellows, I don't want to get off. The world never looked so good to me before.

"Sure—don't worry how you treat the *blacks*. The blacks will do the same to you when they seize power." This is Genêt's message, as far as I'm concerned. *The Blacks* was excellent therapy for many guilt-ridden white folk, which probably explains the long New York run it enjoyed, so much so that many whites went back to see it time and time again. Actually, the so-called "avant-garde" is really a rear-guard action in disguise. It is neither revolutionary, anti-bourgeois, as it sometimes makes pretensions of being, nor anti-white supremacy; it is not even anti-Establishment. It is essentially anti-people. "The West is humanity, humanity is the West, we're all sick to the guts, so let's, man, like all of us get into this here Western style pigsty, and have one final everlasting orgy."

There seems to be a growing tendency in the literature about black and white relationships to give the impression that everything could be solved on the analytical couch. I imagine this approach is a part of the so-called "sexual revolution." The whole "color" thing is merely a deeply rooted psychological sexual complexity and if we could only gather together 190 million black and white Americans into one gargantuan orgiastic group therapy, or perhaps one gigantic therapeutic orgy, all the problems would be solved. I submit that though we might have a ball, after the smoke and funk cleared away, the Great American Problem would still be with us; the Black Man's Burden would not have disappeared. Because the Problem and the Burden are historical, economic, cultural, and social, as well as psychological and sexual. The root of the problem is the Negro Invention.

So now comes the question: Who will uninvent the Negro? For nearly four hundred years the black man's personality has been under attack, his selfhood devastated. Ever since he was brought to this country in chains he has constantly been given the ultimatum: "Deny your humanity or perish!" Where are the artists and prophets who will undo this white destruction? Who will write the songs for us to sing of our black heroes? Who will tell our children of valiant Chalka? Who will recreate the ancient glory that was Timbuktu and Kush and Ghana and Songhay? It is important for us to know that our history on this earth did not begin with slavery's scars.

In order for a people to develop a highly political and revolutionary consciousness, they must hold a high regard for themselves. They must know that they came from *somewhere,* in order to believe themselves capable of going somewhere; they must have a past before they can create a future for themselves. A people needs legends, heroes, myths. Deny them these and you have won half the battle against them.

The French needed legendary figures like Joan of Arc in order to develop a national consciousness, without which any revolution is impossible. So we black folk need Saint Harriet of the Eastern Shore. We must build a literature of heroes, myths, and legends. The lives of Harriet Tubman, Frederick Douglass, Nat Turner, Sojourner Truth, are as formidable as George Washington's, and are based on a much more substantial reality. Our people, young and old, need such heroes desperately. Slavemasters Washington and Jefferson do not belong to *our* children. We need our own myths and legends to regain our lost self-esteem, our regard for each other as a people capable of working together to move the mountains that stand before us. We need such a heritage in order to really believe that we shall prevail.

I'm reminded of a story. A little boy had read numerous stories in his children's books about various life-and-death struggles between a man and lion. But no matter how ferociously the lion fought, each time the man emerged victorious. This puzzled the boy, so he asked his father, "Why is it, Daddy, that in all these stories the man always beats the lion, when everybody knows that the lion is the toughest cat in all the jungle?"

The father answered, "Son, those stories will always end like that until the lion learns how to write."

Few white American writers care enough about the country to criticize it fundamentally. Compared with the ambivalent lot who clutter up the mainstream, they make up a pitifully small pool of courageous talent. Mention James Jones, Norman Mailer, Warren Miller, Lillian Smith, Arthur Miller, Harvey Swados, Ginzburg, Buckmaster, Rosten, Williams, and you have very nearly run out of names. Regardless of how one feels about their views of this society, one must concede that they are writers who care about things deeply. One hopes that one day at least one of them will care deeply enough to dramatize or novelize the white folk who are completely taken in by the "righteous" cause of white supremacy, explain them to us and particularly to themselves in all their myriad contradictions. What is the metamorphosis of a racial bigot? Are they born retarded? Is it fed to them with their mother's milk? The public schools? The press? The church? The mass-communications media? How? Why? When? Where?

America needs to understand what goes into the making of a man who will go out on a Sunday morning in Birmingham, Alabama, and participate in the strange ritual of throwing bombs into a church and killing innocent little Negro children as they are being taught about Jesus, the same Jesus of Nazareth whom the killers profess to worship. And what about the sickness of men who will stand on the sidelines and watch such bloody rituals enacted, without daring to speak? What sort of unspeakable fear has locked their jaws? What is the true anatomy of racial prejudice? Here is a challenge for some writer who cares.

What happens to the dream too long deferred? What white writer will ask America Langston Hughes's question, and come up with some answers? For the dream has been deferred for all the country, black and white. But who will help convince white America that the dream is important to them also? Or have you, too, stopped dreaming? Come on, white brothers. Or don't you really give a damn?

Historically, white America put words in the black man's mouth and bade him sing improbable lyrics like:

> *All the darkies am a-weepin'*
> *Massa's in de cold, cold ground.*

But my great-grandmother told me differently. "We wept all right, honey! Great God A'mighty! We cried for joy and shouted halleluyah!"

Even long after slavery, white America continued the black man singing such banalities as:

> *I got plenty of nuthin'*
> *And nuthin's plenty fo' me.*
>
>   or
>
> *Summertime and the livin' is easy.*

Certainly the American Negro knows, more profoundly than anyone else, that the living is *never* easy.

Even a short while ago, you had us singing:

> *It ain't no sin to dance and grin*
> *That's why darkies were born.*

Yet a black poet once wrote:

> *Carry me back to ol' Virginia—*
> *That's the only way you'll get me there.*

And in our own songs we sang:

> *Sometimes I feel like a motherless child,*
> *A long ways from home.*

We sang:

> *Nobody knows the trouble I see.*

Happy, contented people, we sang:

> *Before I be a slave*
> *I'll be buried in my grave*
> *And go home to my Lord*
> *And be free.*

How did all this begin, this billion-dollar misunderstanding? It started with your determination to have my labor without pay.

In order to justify slavery in a courageous New World spouting slogans of freedom and equality and brotherhood, the enslavers had to create the fiction that the enslaved were sub-human and undeserving of human rights and sympathies. The first job was to convince the outside world of the inherent inferiority of the enslaved. The second job was to convince the American people. And the third job, which was the cruelest hoax of all, was to convince the slaves themselves that they deserved to be the slaves. The propagandists for American slavery (the "creative writers" of that time) tackled their tasks with alacrity and a great measure of success, the effects of which still remain with us today, a hundred years after the Emancipation Proclamation, almost two hundred years after the Declaration of Independence. Thus was the Negro invented and the American Revolution thwarted. To this day, supposedly born in revolution, America is embarrassed by that word. Americans shy away from the word "revolution" like the plague, as if the American Revolution had never happened. Well, did it happen? Knock on any door in Harlem; in all the Harlems of the U.S.A. Ask any black man or woman in Alabama or Mississippi: Was 1776 for real? We black folk are the living proof of whether your revolution was a fake or not.

I attended a party some years ago near the Northwestern University campus, given by some university instructors to celebrate the publication of my first novel, *Youngblood*. One of them told me how much she had enjoyed *Youngblood,* but then asked, "Mr. Killens, do you think you could ever write about people, I mean, not just about Negroes? I mean about people." The nice lady was a trifle flustered.

"You mean, white people, don't you?"

She answered, "Well—yes. I suppose that is what I mean."

"Yes, I believe I could if I wanted to. In fact there are white folk in *Youngblood*. Actually, I believe that a black writer would find it easier writing about white folk than the white writer writing about black folk. The black man has had to know you in order to live in *your* world. I had to know what questions you were going to ask before you asked them, and I had to have the answers ready. But you've always taken me for granted. You come to me with all kinds of pre-conceptions about my innate inferiority. You never get past the myth to the real me."

My rejection slips reveal so much. I've gotten many a "Dear John" in my day, and I still get them.

Dear John:
Thank you for submitting your story to us. It is a powerful and beautiful job. Unfortunately the subject matter is not for us. Frankly, we are not a controversial house.

However, do keep us in mind when you write something else, especially if it has no racial overtones.

Sincerely,

Meaning of course: "John, why do you insist on writing about Negroes? Why don't you write about people?" Why this pressure on the Negro writer to deny his roots? Because the Negro experience in this country is the most fundamental criticism of the American way of life. This reality America has refused to face. It always was and always will be, so long as black remains the symbol of human dispossession. As long as we black folk are D.P.'s in our native land, the controversy will continue to rage. It will always remain a stumbling block in our attempts to win friends and influence people among the African and Asian populations. Africans are concerned with the welfare of their American brothers, and the American brother is becoming more and more concerned with Mother Africa.

Don't write about the Negro, write about Americans. But surely the American Negro is the most uniquely American of all Americans, because he was created *here,* in this place, physically, psychologically, sociologically, culturally, economically. He is an American product. The Negro, in his black presence, is the barometer of this nation's Constitution, and all its democratic traditions yet unrealized. Still deferred. The black man's sojourn in this country is the universal story of man's inhumanity to man, capable of being understood in any language in any nation on the earth. Here is the place for the literary prophets! But maybe Western man is right. "Everything to be said has already been said by Western man." I mean, it may be true that Western man has said all he has to say. It may be that he has run out of meaningful dialogue. God knows, he has talked long enough.

But colored people throughout the world have been sentenced by Western man to centuries of silence. And now in the middle of the twentieth century, it is time for them to speak. Western man wrote his own history as if it were the history of the entire human race. I hope that colored men have watched Western men too long to commit the fatal folly of writing history with a "colored" pencil. For there is a great wisdom in the old Ghana proverb that says: "No one rules forever on the throne of time." Notwithstanding, in this cultural revolution, we must reconstruct the history of the last four hundred years and this time tell *How the West Was Really Won.*

There is much inhumanity, violence, and brutality in our country's history. We must face that. For neither a people nor a nation can free itself from its past by denying or distorting it. White Americans have been sheltered from their history. History is a people's memory, and people have a habit of remembering the very best about themselves. It is an all too human trait. But in the final analysis, a people must face its history squarely in order to transcend it.

3

Downsouth–Upsouth

WE ARE A SOUTHERN COUNTRY, fundamentally. At least for me, Macon, Georgia, where I was born, is "Down South," and New York City, to which I escaped, is "Up South," and the difference is far less than the eight hundred miles that uneasily divide them. And speaking of the supposed difference, I am reminded of a bit of folklore I first heard when I was a boy striving desperately to grow to manhood in the dear old Georgia of my childhood dreams and disillusions. Doubtless it is still going the rounds.

It seems that during the Great Depression a certain hungry soul-brother (African-American) arrived in New York City, freshly escaped from Georgia. Unemployed and destitute and much too nervous to steal, he decided to become a beggar, so he went from house to house along Park Avenue of the Great Affluence. Our hapless hero would knock on the front doors of majestic mansions with hat in hand, and when a door was opened he would go into song-and-dance about his hard luck and his hunger and his mighty awful desperation. Time after time after time, he was told, with profound warmth and courtesy and in all sincerity, and in great sympathy even: "Sorry, sir. We have nothing to give you, sir, but we want you to know in all humility that we wish you all the success in the world, and hope that you will always trust in our Lord and Savior Jesus." Or heartwarming words of Christian brotherhood and fellowship to that effect, which however much it may have warmed the cockles of the brother's heart, did not fill a single nook or cranny of the vacuum in the brother's belly, though it did keep his human dignity intact.

Near the end of his rope (as they used to say, his stomach was beginning to think his throat was cut), he finally knocked on the door of the largest mansion on the street, and a tall, quality-type gentleman came to listen to his sad sad tale. At its conclusion he laughed and said good-naturedly, "All right, nigger, you know better than to be coming to my front door. Go on 'round to the back and tell Mandy I said give you something to eat."

Whereupon the grateful soul-brother replied, "Thank you kindly, suh. You the first Southern gentleman I met since I arrived in New York City!"

We used to laugh at this alleged joke, when we had no better sense. In retrospect, it was undoubtedly concocted by a Southern gentleman from Georgia or Alabama to make the point that the South knew better how to take care of its nigrahs than the North. You see, we Negroes in the South were always a little envious of those uppity, up-the-country Negroes a few years removed from down home, who had managed to shake the red Georgia dust from their feet for the last, last time.

It was a time when some of us were serving advocates *of* and true believers *in* the Southern Way of Life and Southern Womanhood and Segregation, and even lynchings, when they happened, and they very often happened.

Some black brains had been so thoroughly

whitewashed they believed religiously in "our" good white folks, who treated the Negro fairly so long as he stayed in his place, which place was in the most menial of low-paying jobs, in the back of the bus, way up on the last balcony of the movie houses, and in the clapboard segregated one-teacher schoolhouses that covered the southern countryside like the morning dew did dear old Dixie. We believed that rich white folks were good white folks, and poor white trash were bad white folks, which strangely enough contradicted Our Lord and Savior, Jesus Christ, who clearly and on many occasions took a very dim view of the rich man's chances of achieving His Father's Kingdom. And we had good reason, the Holy Bible and Karl Marx's revolutionary working class notwithstanding. For our experience had grimly taught us that the white workingman clung to his whiteness far more desperately than he did to his Christianity and his so-called revolutionary tradition. Was not the white worker the one whom black men saw with the lynch rope in his hand in the cool of a Sunday evening after prayer meeting at the Friendship Tabernacle Church? Was he not the very same man who voted against black membership in the labor unions? Was he not one of the *obvious* reasons that the C.I.O. "Operation Dixie" failed in its noble undertaking to organize the Southern unorganized, the most exploited working class in the country?

When "Operation Dixie" invaded the South, Negros hailed it as the Freedom Train, and they leaped aboard with great enthusiasm and profound dedication. But the train got bogged down very quickly and finally was derailed in the muck and mire of white supremacy. In my home town a Negro church (the one in which I grew up) opened its doors to the organizers (white and black) as a meeting hall. One elderly Negro businessman even jeopardized his life and livelihood by helping the C.I.O. organize the unorganized, though this had nothing to do directly with him or his business, but being black he realized it had everything to do with him, or should have. A couple of years before he died he said to me: "Son, there ain't no colored or no Negro problem in the land. The color of the problem is pure-dee white. It's the white folks that ain't ready yet."

When white and black labor organizers came to Macon, they paid nightly visits to Negro homes and talked to black folk about the union, but practically nobody talked to the white workers; to tackle those poor, misguided, brainwashed bastards would have been to touch them at their tenderest spot, their racial prejudices. To do so would have challenged the Southern Way of Life at its foundations. The C.I.O.'s "Operation Dixie," like Reconstruction, indeed like the American Revolution and every other American movement that should have spelled freedom and equality for Americans of all colors and religions, died still-born. To give the C.I.O. its due, it did not keep the Negroes *out*. The trouble was it could not keep the white workers *in*.

Well-to-do white folk, actually, have always confused the Southern Negro. They have always been to the black man like the dog that wags his tail and growls simultaneously. One is hard put to know which end to believe. We do know, though, that the well-heeled Mister Charlies control the jobs of working people, black and white, and also the Southern mass-communications media. And therefore, in a real sense, they control the minds of poor white Southerners. We also know that historically they have parlayed the racial prejudices of the poor whites vis-à-vis Negroes into a profitable system of divide-and-rule that has, in plain words, meant cheap non-union labor. Ask any honest labor organizer who hoed the union row in Dixie.

During the great race riot in Atlanta near the beginning of the century, wealthy white folks stripped their own "house niggers" and took their clothes and locked them in their rooms and then went out and killed other Negroes on the streets of Atlanta.

The pragmatic philosophy of some Negroes, particularly in the smaller Southern towns, used to be: "The way for a black man to get along is to attach himself to some well-to-do *good* white folks. Just one big white folks is all you need. Then don't care what happen, can't nobody do you no big harm. Not the sheriff, police, judge, *nobody!* Not even the Good Lord Up on High!"

Nobody but the good white folks, that is. I remember as a boy walking the streets of my home town one night when a big black Packard drove up alongside me with two well-appointed white gentlemen in the front seat and stopped. One of them leaned out and beckoned me over. "Hey, boy, you know where we can get a colored gal?"

I yelled, "Go get your dear old mother like you been doing!" and ran, with tears in my eyes. Angrily I wished to God I'd been a grown man that night, but at the same time I was relieved that I was only ten years old and didn't have to assert my manhood. Even at that age, I felt the sharp denial of my manhood. And that is another thing the struggle between the black man and his country is all about, his manhood, his black manhood, which has been denied him ever since he was brought here in slavery.

Two summers ago, in a little sleepyhead cot-

ton-center town in Dixie, a white man walked up
to a black man and his black wife and shot the
husband down dead in full view of the momentari-
ly startled pedestrians. The only words that
passed between them came from the self-righteous
white man who said, just before he pulled the
trigger, "Nigger, didn't I tell you to stay away
from this black woman?"

This was, no doubt, in the proud tradition of
protecting Southern womanhood. This is how the
white man has so nobly fought miscegenation. In
any event, for one brief moment the town awoke,
then went immediately back to sleep again. The
brave gunfighter was inconvenienced for two or
three hours at the county jail and then—*case
closed.*

During the days of slavery the black man was
given another ultimatum: "Deny your manhood
or die!" And ever since we were brought here
in chains we have been cast in the role of eunuchs
in a great white harem. But now, at this historic
moment, "Down South" and "Up South," we
refuse to be your eunuchs any longer.

I remember the first day I came to Washington,
D.C., from the Deep South. I was nineteen years
old, with the great American success story exud-
ing from my every pore and glowing in my eyes,
however tentatively. Life is tentative for most people, but especially for Negroes. We never look

a gift horse in the mouth, but we have learned to keep an eye on it from other vantage points. Like hoboes, metaphorically speaking, we always sleep with one eye open. I had been called by my government to work in the nation's capital, which I somehow imagined to be the freest place on earth. But even my young naïve imagination had more sense than that. Nevertheless, I would be working in the White House, and I had high hopes. Never mind that it was only a messenger's job, it was in the White House.

Now let me state here categorically: I was never in the White House in my entire life. But to the innocent, unsophisticated Southlander, Washington was just one great big White House, and everybody who left Dixie to go to work for the government in Washington was going to work in the White House. Even colored people. My older brother was already working in the White House, at the Government Printing Office more than a mile away.

When I walked into the file room that first Monday morning and announced that I was John Oliver Killens, a tall white boy from New York City thrust his hand toward me for a friendly handshake. As I recall, my split-second reaction (conditioned reflex) was to throw up my guard or duck my head, believing that young "Whitey" was going to hit me for being arrogant and sassy, or for no particular reason at all. There never had to be a reason. In any event I was very slow on the draw, downright backward really, it being the first time a white man had offered his hand to me or ever called me "Mister" Killens.

I was the only Negro working at the National Labor Relations Board, and all day long I walked around the place wondering where the drinking fountain and the toilet were—*For Colored,* that is. I was too proud to ask my white colleagues and lacked the courage to take anything for granted, especially white folk. It was a part of my upbringing to take nothing for granted when it came to the schizophrenic ways of white folk.

It was about four in the sweaty afternoon before necessity and sheer desperation dictated that I go for broke and damn the consequences. Of course there were no drinking or toilet facilities exclusively *For Colored.* There had been no occasion for them, since I was one of those peculiarities in the life of Black America known as a "First Negro," notwithstanding my humble messenger status, which is pretty hysterical when you come to ponder on it. Such humiliating experiences are certainly not unique in the context of American Negro experience, and hardly worth mentioning. But how many red-blooded, all-American white boys ever experience this particular kind of lynching of the human spirit, this psychological castration?

It was on my first trip back to Macon that I realized more sharply than ever before, the chasm between the Northern and the Southern Negro, built on myth and misconceptions on both sides of the Mason-Dixon Line. Under the impact of the Negro Revolt, this chasm is slowly disappearing, but it was real and wide and deep in those days of not so long ago. I had been in Washington no more than six or seven months when my older brother and I drove back at the end of that first summer.

Everybody put on the dog for us; most everybody also put up a wall between *them* and *us*. Most of the boys and girls I'd grown up with, all of my buddies with whom I had spent my childhood swimming naked in the muddy Ocmulgee River, had laughed and played and cried and cussed and dreamed with, most of them now looked upon me as a stranger. To them, I was an agent from an alien land spying on them. By my very presence I was an unspoken accusation, as if I were actually challenging each and every one of them: "Why in the hell haven't you had the gumption to leave this hell-hole like I did?"

Consequently, when you asked one of your best friends an innocuous question like "How's every little thing?" he went out of his way to assure you that nobody ever had it so good. He pointed to his automobile, his new home on the outskirts of town. He exaggerated the progress that had been made since you left, as if you'd been away for ages. The new mayor and the sheriff were good white folks. Things were different from what they used to be. Never once did he let you get beneath the thin layer of his insecurity, brought about immediately upon hearing you were back in town. You knew what he .was thinking: "Lording it over everybody, hasn't been up North long enough to get his feet wet, and already he's talking with a brogue."

In retrospect, there was at least some superficial truth in this reaction. One of the first things a Southern Negro did upon moving farther North was to begin work on losing his Southern accent, the symbol of the near-slave status he had just put behind him, forever, he hoped. This losing of our "Southernness" was a defense mechanism of us latecomers to the North against that rarity of the species, the Northern-born Negro, or against Negroes who had taken off their Southern shoes one whole year ahead of us.

In those days most Negroes were fiercely ashamed of their Southern background, so much so, that it amounted to an inferiority complex. My first year in the Army, during the late World-Wide Madness, I was the company clerk for a segregated company. Not a single one of the men in my outfit admitted being from Georgia or Alabama or Mississippi. They were all from Chicago, Cleveland, Detroit, or New York, and you wondered about the very Southern accents they carried with them, dogging their heels, belying their "birthplace." You wondered, that is, until you looked at their files and found that Billy Joe Washington was indeed from Cleveland, though he had been there for at most two or three weeks before he was drafted, having spent the remainder of his twenty-two years in Yazoo City, Mississippi. The same applied to J. B. Jones, from Georgia via New York City, and Victor Jackson, who had been in Chicago a scant three months after escaping from Chittling Switch, Alabama.

Each time I went South, the chasm widened, though it is probable that it did not deepen, since the chasm, after all, was superficial. After the war, I went back with my Northern wife and children. The number of my schoolmates who had remained in Macon had dwindled considerably. A few had offered up their lives as sacrifices in the great bloodletting, and the Jim Crow American Legion post was named after one of them. Others had remained in Paris after the war, or stopped off on their way home in New York or Chicago or Detroit or Los Angeles, and never made it back. But those who did come back stayed; they built landscaped ranch-type houses and bought bigger automobiles and became more and more defensive vis-à-vis the Northern Negro.

I often felt like saying: "Look, fellows, remember me? I'm the same guy you grew up with. You don't have to prove anything to me, any more than I have to prove anything to you. Who is to say which took more courage? To stay with the South and fight it out here, or to give up and migrate to the North like D.P.'s in time of war?"

Negroes in Northern ghettoes often lived in a fool's paradise, and somehow the Southern Negro knew it and resented it. Many Northern Negroes thought they had it made, no matter what their circumstances, merely because they were up North. They felt a condescending pity for their downtrodden brother in the South, but they no longer felt the same bond of mutual suffering and exploitation. In a way it was an extension of the Southern "good white folks" myth. Everything in this dialogue was based on the attitudes of white folks, "good" or "bad," "Crackers" or "Northerners." White folks were still the determining factor. And what the Southern Negro said in rebuttal was at least partially true. "You raggedy-ass Negroes up there in Harlem and on the South side of Chicago living on top of each other in the company of rats and bedbugs, what you got to be so high and mighty about? You got freedom all right—freedom to starve to death. What if you can go to them ·hotels downtown? Hell, you can't even afford the subway fare!"

Once when I was in Montgomery, Alabama, as a guest of the vice president of Alabama State Teachers College, his wife told me, "We often thought about moving North, but in the final analysis we decided it didn't make that much difference. Whenever we visited New York and looked up our old friends, we found most of them living in Harlem, just as segregated as they'd ever been, and just as far away from the cultural life of New York—the theater and Carnegie Hall—as they'd been when they lived in Alabama. All they'd done was travel hundreds of miles to settle in another Southern community. We see more of Broadway on our visits than they do their whole life through."

It must be said that when the ex-Southern Negro returned home for a visit he was also on the defensive. He had to give the impression that he had done well up North. So when he was there he usually showed up at church on Sunday, even though in New York he never attended, and wearing the latest style in clothing. He showed off his Northern brogue, which was oftentimes an unknowing caricature of the real thing, and he might even have borrowed somebody's big long Cadillac to drive down in. But notwithstanding, the differences between the black brothers and sisters, North and South, were always superficial. The ties were never broken fundamentally; the Northern Negro still had family ties and friendships back home. Richard Wright was never closer to the truth than when he spoke of the irreducible strength of familial love, which transcended all the white man's laws and conventions. Despite the eternal, unabating pressure on the black man to hate the face he stares at in his mirror, his love for his black brother has survived.

I remember when I was a lad in Macon, you would hear that a funeral was going to be on Thursday, then Friday, then Saturday or Sunday, and then it might finally take place on the following Tuesday or Wednesday. What was happening was that the family was waiting for its members to gather from the far corners of the land. And so long as there was hope that a brother or a sister or even a distant cousin would make it, the funeral would be postponed again and again.

A family very close to mine, when I was about eight years old, lost one of its members. It was winter and a cold one for our part of the country; snow lay on the land from the Great Lakes all the way to Jacksonville. One of the brothers of the deceased was living in Chicago as was one of his sisters. He had come upon hard times and was penniless. But he borrowed enough money from his sister to get his clothes and suitcases out of hock and checked the bags on her ticket. She rode the train as a passenger; he rode the boxcars. At Atlanta, where it was necessary to change trains, he got his bag and went into the colored restroom to bathe, shave, and put on his best suit, then caught the same train to Macon with his sister. The people in Macon shook their heads.

"That boy sure did prosper up the country!"

Now, lest the wrong impression be given, there were always some Southern Negroes who had no need to be defensive, had no good white folks to speak of, and always spoke their minds and told it like it was. One of them told me a fantastic (true) story about a young man who had come back from the Second World-Wide Madness, and built up a promising vegetable trucking business. He was married and had a couple of children, and through industry and faith in free enterprise had built up a fairly successful business. Each day he would drive his truck out to the edge of town where the farmers' markets were to buy produce and bring it back to the neighborhood to sell.

One morning he was on his way to the market

in his truck when the white driver of an automobile tried to take the highway away from him. The young veteran would not relinquish his position, a few words were passed, and they both went their contemplative ways. He arrived at the first market and exchanged greetings with his friend the wholesale produce man, a real sensitive friendly type good white man, who didn't hold anything against the Negro simply because he was a Negro. Besides it was good business to be friendly to young prospering Negroes. After all, you didn't have to invite them into your home.

"Morning, Mr. Henry," the young black ex-G.I. said pleasantly.

"Morning, Joe," the chubby produce man replied, with equal pleasantness. "Excuse me for a minute, I'll be back directly."

"All right, Mr. Henry."

While Mr. Henry was inside for one hot minute, the white driver appeared and, leaping from his car, jumped G.I. Joe, shouting insults about "goddamn biggedy niggers." By the time Mr. Henry came back outside, Joe and the white man were rolling in the dust. Rushing back into the store, he reappeared with his pistol and shot Joe as dead as he had to be to die. That's right, killed his "friend" and cash customer, even though he'd never seen this white man before in his entire life.

One thing the Negro Revolt has taught the Negro, North and South, is the universality of his degradation, that so long as human dignity is denied him in one section of this country, he will never achieve it fully in the other. Such wisdom was not always with us.

And now it should be said, lest someone gets a false impression, we black folk do not spend twenty-four hours of each day musing over the ways of white folks. Believe it or not, our time is much too valuable. When we leave the white man's job, most of us *really* leave the white man's job. We go home to another life which is black and has dignity, and though we may be the janitor in your apartment building or an elevator operator or the cleaner of your streets, we are leaders in our own communities. Club presidents and trustees and deacons and elders and Grand Exalted Rulers. As much as it is possible, we shut your alien white life out of our hearts and souls and minds. Every evening we leave the foreign country, and we go home to our families, our associations, our Grand Lodges, our societies, our Elks, our Masons, our churches. The Negro Revolt notwithstanding, our main involvement is with ourselves, not with white folk, not even with integration, which you believe to be our obsession. It may hurt some white folk's tender sensitivities to hear this, but the truth is most Negroes could not care less about integrating with most white folk. We are not so uncritical, having lived in a society among a people that has denied us for nearly four hundred years. There must be something basically sick about such a society or something basically wrong with us, and loving us, as we do, we favor the former.

When I listen to my people's songs, when I feel the beauty and the strength and the depth of their feelings, when I ponder over the essential hard-working goodness of my people, along with the human weaknesses which are common to all men; as I have shed my own tears and heard my own laughter, just as I have felt their tears and heard their laughter, which is mine and mine theirs, for in the deepest sense our hopes and aspirations are one and indivisible; as I ponder all these things, I raise this question: How could you, who claim to be the land that spawned the basic rights of man, deny an entire people such as we? We upon whose backs the nation's initial wealth was accumulated?

There is something wrong here, fundamentally wrong. That is why we don't aspire merely to reach where you stand now on sinking sand. We want to move the whole country to higher ground and build a society that will make sense for all the people, black and white. We want freedom and we will be free. And integration and freedom are not synonymous, certainly not in *our* dictionary. Freedom is a principle men have historically laid down their lives for; integration with dignity for the integrated can only come after the fact of freedom.

Another thing. You are forever buying off us "different" ones, but the price is never right. The offer never includes manhood or freedom. Historically, the reward has been, and still is, merely to graduate to "house niggers," to be grateful for the crumbs from old Massa's table. And in compensation for this we must play the role of Gunga Din. This is what is still expected, be it Down South or Up South, of every "different," "educated" Negro.

When I was an undergraduate at Morris Brown College in Atlanta, I remember vividly the "integrated" forums we used to attend of a Sunday afternoon over on the Atlanta University (or the Morehouse or Spellman) campus. There would usually be a few students from Georgia Tech and Emory (both very-lily-and-very-very-white at the time), but most of us were from the surrounding Negro colleges.

We black people, whether we come from the city or village or the country farms of Georgia, are rarely ever more than one generation removed from a peasant background, a background very close to the soil and fraught with deprivation. Yet most of our parents instilled in us a kind of nervous and precarious dignity and a blind faith in the American dream, to wit: "If you persevered and prepared yourself, you would be ready to go inside the door of success when opportunity knocked." If the metaphor were badly mixed, it was probably because the reasoning was terribly mixed up and the dream itself had little or nothing to do with the American reality.

At most of these forums we inevitably and interminably discussed how to rid the country of the "Problem." What else was there for black and white students to discuss together on a college campus in Atlanta on a Sunday afternoon? One Sunday afternoon I remember in particular. The speaker (white and aristocratic-looking) had finished, and questions had been coming from the floor for three-quarters of an hour when a tall, blonde, crew-cut boy from Emory or Georgia Tech got to his feet and proclaimed to one and all that he had *the* solution to the "nigrah" problem. We all waited with bated breath, as the cliché goes.

"The way to get rid of the nigrah problem," he said gravely, "is to collect all the nigrahs together and take them to the river and dump them in."

There was shocked silence. But well, he wore a serious expression, you know. He wasn't making with the joke. And he appeared to be perfectly sober.

On another Sunday afternoon we were lectured at by a charming white professor from one of the liberal, white, Southern colleges. And afterward, as we stood outside on the campus 'neath the falling shadows of a dying day in autumn, he approached a group of about five of us young colored "elite," who gathered around him expectantly as he let us in on the great big secret. "You fellows are all right," he said. "You're different, you're not like the rest of them. It's the riff-raff over on Decatur Street that makes things hard for the rest of you-all." And we all felt properly superior and smiled our dazzling dark smiles at this magnanimous great white father. He had knighted us, and we were properly grateful. He even almost shook our hands.

The funny thing about the South, more alarming than hilarious, is that they believed their own propaganda. They believed in the reality of their happy nigrahs. They created the myth and came to believe in it religiously, making it into a way of life. And that is the scary part. That is the sickness.

During the Montgomery Bus Protest Movement, I spent some time in the "Cradle of the Confederacy." I witnessed a growing realization, a deep sense of disillusionment among the white folk, that something was wrong with their own "dyed-in the-wool-happy-and-contented-Dixie-nig-rahs."

One elderly red-necked poor white man summed it up to a Negro newsman from the North: "I just can't understand it. Here we were minding our own business, and the races gittin' along together separately, they on they side of the street and us on ourn, and then one day *boom!* All this bus-boycott business and carrying on!"

The old man scratched and shook his scraggly head, rather in the manner of Stepin Fetchit or Willie Best. His old face wore a puzzled expression. "It's like fifty thousand other nigrahs moved into town under cover of darkness and took the places of our nigrahs. They look like our nigrahs, but Lord in Heaven knows they sure don't act like them!"

And all over the South today, with the demonstrations, white men look at their own Southern nigrahs with a hurt sense of deep betrayal. Black folk are no longer speaking their lines according to the old script, and this is disquieting. "When you can't rely on your own nigrahs, what is this old world coming to? It makes you lose faith in human nature, not that nigrahs are human, necessarily."

And yet it is difficult for a Negro raised in the South to put that part of the country irrevocably behind him. It is not easy to leave a place where you have lived out the days of your childhood, when all your memories have not been those of ugliness. You do remember the soft quiet beauty of a Southern town, which is unmatched by the crowded, noisy, soot-filled urban centers of the North. You do remember the fragrance of honeysuckle and magnolias. You do remember going barefoot in the early Southern springs that come when blankets of snow still lie over most of the Northern country, and the clouds of birds that filled the sky coming South and going further South. You recall the lazy hot summer days when there was a greenness over everything and the smell of the Georgia pines standing tall and lording it over the rest of the forest. And that was good. You have memories of going for hikes into the woods and picking wild blackberries and muscadines and going swimming out the "Big Road" in an infamously treacherous swimming hole on the sly and getting a whipping when you got home because you forgot to dry your hair. And Sunday-school picnics that always came in May, the long tables of food and ice-cold lemonade and the games played and the romping and tearing about as if nobody ever had a care in the world. You even remember the teachers in the segregated schools who seemed "mean" and "strict," because they cared, the whipping you got at school or the ones your parents gave you when you got home with the note saying you hadn't done your best. Everybody cared, everybody believed in you and in your capacity as a human being, and you belonged to everybody, so everybody was determined that you do your very best. This is the kind of loving care a black child misses almost entirely in the "integrated" schools Up South in New York City, where most of the teachers are white, and many of them could not care less whether you are prepared for the future, or even if you have a future. This is the great contradiction in the fight for "integrated" schools. Negro children often find themselves in a school system where nobody seems to give a damn, and discipline is almost wholly for precious discipline's sake.

I went, a couple of years ago, to an "Open School Week," and overheard a Brooklyn high-school teacher tell a worried Negro parent, "I wouldn't worry about Jerry, Mrs. Wilson. He's doing all right, about as well as could be expected. He's a nice boy, doesn't give anyone any trouble. We don't have any disciplinary problems with Jerry at all."

"But," the frustrated mother protested, "I am not worried about his deportment, I'm worried about his grades. I know he can do better."

"Everybody thinks his child can do better, Mrs. Wilson."

In the "integrated" schools, too many of the symbols of authority are white, almost all the principals and assistants, most of the teachers. There are only two Negro school principals in the whole of New York City. If integration is to have any real meaning for black children, integration must be achieved at the level of authority, as well as in the student body. I mean black and white kids must experience some black authority. How can there be incentive without example?

Are all Northern white teachers antagonistic to their Negro students? No. There are a few who care. I have known a precious few. My son has also, as has my daughter. I have heard of others. But they are the exceptions that prove overwhelmingly what the rule might be, but isn't.

Yes, it's easy to be nostalgic about a Southern childhood, Christmas mornings when black folk went from house to house, knocking on doors, and when the doors were opened, crying, "Christmas gift!" Then the answer: "Hand it here!"

And this from those who had nothing to give but the gift of giving. You remember Easter mornings when you gathered on the hill (even a few "good" white folks gathered to the side of you), and sang songs of Jesus' crucifixion and of his triumph over the grave and watched the sunrise shout for joy for Mary's boy-child and his Resurrection.

Or going home on a train, leaving Washington with the snow lying quiet over everything but beginning to vanish as you moved deeper into Virginia, then North Carolina and its faint hint of springtime and South Carolina where spring had already arrived, and finally the red clay hills of North Georgia, with the tall pine trees glistening in the warm sunlight. You remembered suddenly all the good things about your home, and it *was* home, after all, no matter how violently you denied it. And you got a choking in your throat of sweet nostalgia.

Then the not-so-sweet reality as the train dashed by the little country stations with red-neck Crackers sitting outside staring at the world passing them by forever, with black men standing to the side, always to the side, staring too, but with a different look, and then all at once you became aware of the little outhouses alongside the stations with the signs that reminded you in bold crude letters: FOR WHITE ONLY.

So you were brought sharply back to the truth about your dear old honeysuckled Southland. Whatever the natural beauty of this land, it was a superficial beauty; it had the prettiness of a lovely woman with the insides of a hard-hearted whore. And you wept inside for what it could be but never had been, and you began to wonder if it ever would. You're sometimes seized with a helpless anger at the sickness of this beautiful bitch. She could be beautiful inside. You knew she could be. But, Good Lord, would she ever, as long as she pretended that she was already the mostest of the very most?

And yet the hope is always there with many black folk that the South shall one day lead the nation. She has misled us all these years since Reconstruction. This is what makes them stay with the South and struggle with her redemption. The hope that the few white folk who care will increase steadily and gain more courage from our display of black courage so that no longer will they let the loudmouthed ones intimidate them. The desperate hope that there are many more white folk "ready" than black folk dare suspect. It is this that gives the Freedom Riders such fierce conviction when they sing: "We shall overcome some day."

But white allies or no, we black folk mean to overcome.

We are a Southern country, not incidentally, but fundamentally, and the sooner we acknowledge this, the sooner we will be able to get down to the business of changing. This is, after all, what the demonstrating is all about, including the Freedom Rides, the Sit-Ins, Malcolm X, James Farmer, the Wade-Ins, Daisy Bates, the Harlem Riot, Rochester, Jersey City, Bedford-Stuyvesant, Roy

Wilkins, John Lewis, Rosa Parks, Whitney Young, and Jackson, Mississippi. The purpose is to change and thereby save the country, not to help the "poor downtrodden colored man."

Reconstruction is the purpose. Ours has been a racist-oriented country from the beginning. Even in the days of slavery, the vaunted North was Southern country. The slaves knew this—or found it out very soon. A fugitive slave learned he was never really free until he crossed over into Canada. If he had not known this beforehand, the Dred Scott decision made everything very clear. The Supreme Court said, in essence: "No black man had a right that any white man need respect." This is the brutal truth of our history which we must transcend. We are, black and white, still the slaves of our history, of the myths as against the historical reality.

Up South in New York City, in Chicago and Detroit and Los Angeles, in all the Northern urban centers, black folk face *de facto* segregation and discrimination and other denials of basic humanity. These denials are sharp and hard and fast and real. They all spell human exploitation; economic, political, social, cultural. This harsh reality is all the crueler for the millions of words of lip service paid by Northern mouths to equality and brotherhood. In the Deep South they do not celebrate "Brotherhood Week." In the North they invented "Brotherhood Week," and that is one of the basic differences between New York and Atlanta.

Dick Gregory has said: "The only difference between the Negro in the North and the Negro in the South is that the Negro is a little safer (physically) in the North." Well, at least he's safer from the whims of the average white civilian. In New York his most obvious adversary is often the "Finest." I suspect that the police play a similar role in most Northern cities. Only the most brain-washed of Negroes in Harlem or other Northern ghettos *really* believe that the police are in their community to protect them. The age-old cry in Harlem is: "Who will protect us from the representatives of law and order?" Let's face it. We Negroes did not invent the "myth of police brutality."

If this be paranoia, it evolves from our black reality. To most Negroes the "friendly cop" is a contradiction in terms. To most of us the police in the black ghetto are the army of occupation, Storm Troopers, U.S.A., protectors of the *status quo* which has always been anathema to our black existence. The point is: Whether Colonel Penn was gunned to death on a Georgia highway by the K.K.K., or fifteen-year-old Powell shot by one of New York's "Finest," the fact is, neither killer will be brought to task by the enforcers of law and order. Everybody knows it. And almost everybody accepts it. There is the sickness.

Where are your law and order that you ask the "hoodlums" of Harlem to respect? Where is your boasted justice, when I can say, and honestly, that so far as I know no white man has *ever* been capitally punished for murdering a Negro in America. Repeat more calmly: No white man has ever paid the supreme penalty for killing one of us, North, South, East, or West, so far as I have been able to determine.

The ghettoes of the North are as firmly entrenched in the urban centers as they are in any Southern city. They are citadels of black despair, a despair that expresses itself in dope addiction, alcoholism, the numbers racket, school drop-outs, juvenile delinquency, teen-age gang warfare, crime and prostitution, and more positively in occasional riots. It is a curious thing the way most Northern newspapers designated the Harlem rioters as hoodlums, while the rioters on the beaches of New Hampshire and Oregon were merely pranksters, students, high-spirited youngsters. Psychologists were quoted in *The New York Times* as saying that the young people who ran amuck on the fancy beaches of America last Labor Day were in "quest of their identity." Well, is there a youth who has been more deprived of his identity than the youth of Harlem? I honestly believe, though I say this with all kinds of trepidation, that the Harlem riot was a healthy thing for the country and for Harlem. The wonder is that it took so long for our patience to wear thin.

The fight for this country's emancipation must be successful in the Northern cities if the struggle in Jackson, Mississippi, and St. Augustine, Florida, is to have any real significance. What are we fighting for in the South? Merely to become like the North?

We, as a people, at this moment in the twentieth century, must determine once and for all which shall have primacy in our land, the sanctity of private property or the dignity of man. This is the question colored peoples all over the world are posing for the twentieth century. This is the truer, deeper meaning of the Negro Revolt. The Negro is the conscience of the Western world. There can be no American morality without affirmation of black human dignity. There can be only immorality and decadence.

Of course one must say now emphatically, the North is not the South. New York is not Mississippi. Negroes *can* sit at the front of the Northern buses and eat hot dogs at Nedick's or Chock Full o' Nuts counter. Black men and women can register and vote without imminent danger to life or limb, and only disenchantment and hopelessness keep black folk from flocking to the polls in greater numbers. In the final analysis, we Negroes must pool our strength and turn our despair into hope and human dignity. We have too often put the cart before the horse. Moving into a white neighborhood cannot be the solution for the mass of black city dwellers. Negroes themselves, against overwhelming odds, must make the ghetto livable, a fitting place to raise our children. We must make the Harlems of the U.S.A. sources of black strength, political and otherwise. For as my son, Chuck, wrote me after exposure to the Negro community of Washington: "I suddenly realized that the Negro ghetto is not a ghetto. It is home."

It is time for black folk to de-brainwash themselves. Too long we have accepted the psychology that anything that was all black was *ipso facto* inferior. It is a psychology of self-hatred and self-destruction.

Harlem is home to hundreds of thousands of black folk. Harlem is many things other than dope addiction and prostitution. Harlem is people; freedom-loving people, loving freedom so fiercely because of their denial of it. Hard-working, unemployed; alert, apathetic; hopeful, despairing; proud, lazy, and industrious people; Democrats, Republicans; radicals, liberals, even one or two reactionaries.

Harlem is E. Franklin Frazier's *Black Bour-*

geoisie in Lenox Terrace and in Riverton, respectable and striving. Harlem has recently been the protagonist of many a book and magazine article, and invariably it has turned out to be the antagonist, the eternal anti-hero. More often than not, Harlem is pictured as one vast "jungle" unsafe for human habitation; the established Western image being that a jungle is inhabited by wild animals and savages, plus a few courageous white men, missionaries and such, who brave the jungle at their own peril to "civilize and Christianize the natives." And the worst of it was, that what was said of Harlem by outsiders, many Harlemites believed. But Harlem is, among other things, a city of True Believers, including striving, middle-class believers in the sanctity of free enterprise and church-going, God-fearing people who foresee a better life for their children and still buy the American dream. Harlem is the 135th Street Y.M.C.A. and the new Y.W. on 125th Street. Harlem is the Countee Cullen Library and the famed Schomburg Collection. Harlem is raw black anger, black frustration, disillusionment. Harlem is HARYOU, which could spell hope for Harlem children. Harlem is Black Nationalism. Harlem is Muslims. Harlem is bars and funeral parlors and black laughter and Langston Hughes and Malcolm X and Nipsey Russell and Adam Powell and Jesse Gray and Percy Sutton. Harlem is way Up North, the Promised Land. Carl Van Vechten once called it "Nigger Heaven."

Yet Harlem is, for all that, essentially Dixie accents and Southern attitudes, like every acre of the North, shackled forever to the South. Abe Lincoln once said that "no nation can remain half-free and half-slave." Nor can a country remain half-North and half-South. That is why we must all get down to business. And un-South the entire nation. Now is the time.

4

The Myth of
Non-Violence
versus
The Right of Self-Defense

THE ONE THING most of the friends and all of the enemies of the American Negro have agreed upon is that black folk in the U.S.A. are by nature non-violent, and that they should forever remain as God and nature ordained them.

And so a new myth about the Negro is being perpetrated throughout the land. Along with the old myths of laziness and cunning, stupidity and irresponsibility, sexual prowess-and-obsession and all the others, tried and trusted, is being added the new myth of non-violence. In the middle of the twentieth century, when the disinherited all over the earth are on the move in affirmation of their manhood, the world is being sold a bill of goods, that America has evolved a new type of Homo sapiens, the Non-Violent Negro. In this era of automation and cybernetics, we should be highly suspicious of all such evolutionary claims. This new type, if he does indeed exist, might very well be the result of an immaculate conception, the absolute purity of which man and legend never imagined. He was most probably conceived by an impeccable computer, and has no relationship whatever to the order of the Primates.

As I have said elsewhere, one of the basic denials eternally experienced by the black man in America has been the suppression of his manhood. I believe one of the first songs I ever heard Harry Belafonte sing was one he wrote himself, "Recognition as a Man."

When I was in Bamako, the capital of the Republic of Mali in West Africa, in 1961, a white friend who worked at the American Embassy warned me over drinks to beware of the Malians. "Don't be caught out alone after dark," he cautioned me. "These people are very anti-American. They will visit all manner of indignities upon you."

Me? Indignities upon me?

I cracked up with laughter, and my friend's pale face reddened.

"What the hell are you laughing about?"

"The joke is on both of us, buddy," I said.

"What are you talking about?"

"If you don't know already, how can I explain it to you?"

What had brought on my laughing jag was a kind of sadistic, masochistic sense of humor that comes over me in certain situations. What struck me as hilariously funny, in a masochistic sort of way, was that I had had to travel thousands of miles away from my native land to suddenly become an American. At home I was a "nigger." And I had been walking the downtown streets of Bamako just the night before alone at two in the morning (the streets are dark and empty in Bamako at 2 A.M.), feeling no apprehension, musing over how different I would have felt had I been walking certain streets of my own home town, Macon, Georgia, where I had lived as a boy but could never grow up to be a man, black manhood being a hazardous pursuit in Macon, Georgia, Jackson, Mississippi, or Birmingham, Alabama, as any Freedom Rider or Sit-In Student will attest, and as every Negro knows instinctively.

Now one of the basic attributes of manhood (when we say manhood, we also mean womanhood, selfhood) is the right of self-defense. In the systematic, psychological castration of the Negro, which has continued unabated ever since he was brought here in chains from Africa, the deprivation of this right has been one of the most effective instruments. Madame Simone de Beauvoir was most apt in her analogy between the training of girls for womanhood in a bourgeois society and the pressures brought to bear on American Negroes to know their place and stay forever in it.

Both represent the same kind of self-denial, the self-same human abnegation, though in the case of the American Negro the training is a hundred times as single-minded and purposeful. To grind down black men bit by bit and turn them into eunuchs is the purpose of the process. It begins in Dixie at a very tender age.

I was born on Virgin Street, at the edge of a white upper-middle-class neighborhood. On our way to school we black kids had to pass through this neighborhood, which consisted of great colonial mansions, two and three stories tall, and awesome, set in the midst of huge, majestic oak trees. Some of the grounds seemed more like college campuses. Each day on the way to *our* school and back we crossed paths with white children bound for *their* school.

It didn't help our black dispositions any that our "separate-but-equal" wooden frame school buildings were a paint-peeled tattletale gray, featuring outhouses without running water. They didn't even have water that stood still. It didn't help much to realize that white kids went to school in modern brick buildings with inside toilets and all the other comforts of sanitation. They had the services of janitors and charwomen, we had to do the cleaning up ourselves. In the winter they had steam heat, while we had only pot-bellied stoves with a pan of water on top. One of our wise-ass kids said one cold day in January: "How come you complain so much? We got steam heat. Can't you see that pan of water steaming?"

One spring, which came quite early that year as it usually does in Georgia, an incident erupted at the crossroads. A white lad called a Negro boy that word, I mean the one white folk invented the better to castrate us black Americans.

Innocently enough he asked, "Hey, nigger, what you learn in school today?" Friendly-like.

"I learned your mother was a whore," the sassy black boy answered. We were all seven to eleven years old.

His black buddies laughed appreciatively, the white boy slapped his face, and that was how it started. Everybody got into the act. We fist-fought, we rock-battled, we laid on each other with sticks and baseball bats, and everything else that came to hand. Nobody won, and after a while it just sort of petered out. We black kids went home with cut lips and bloody noses, but we went home proud and happy, though we got our backsides whipped for tearing our school clothes. By the next day we had forgotten it.

But just before noon the school ground swarmed with police. They strode into classrooms without even a "Good morning" to the teachers and dragged out scared kids, many of them crying. They even dragged them out of the outhouses and snatched them as they tried to flee the school ground. They took some who had been in the "riot" and a number who'd never even heard about it. Somehow they missed yours truly. I felt left out and rejected, insulted even, especially since I was the bosom buddy of the kid who had started it.

Then frightened black mothers were brought down to the jailhouse to whip their children in front of the policemen to teach them not to fight white children. The alternative was the reformatory, though not a single white child was rounded up. Thus they drove the lesson home, the lesson that every black American must learn one way or another: that he has no inalienable right to defend himself from attack by Mister Charlie; that even though he can expect his own black person to be violated at any moment, he must remember better than anything else in this world that the white man's person is inviolable so far as he is concerned. The cruelest aspect of this story is how they used black mothers to drive this lesson home.

Negro men have walked with their wives through the streets of Southern towns and had to pretend they did not hear the sexual insults directed at their wives by white men, because to admit you heard meant you had to react as any man must react, bringing down the wrath of white folks upon your head, and indeed putting your black life on the line. To take issue with *one* white man was to fight the entire white establishment. And it mobilized in a hurry. Sure, it's a slow and easy kind of life in the sunny Southland, but some things can happen in a hurry.

Take Plum Nelly, Georgia, even in the 1960's —*A Fine Place to Raise Your Children,* the sign says. Barnum and Bailey has come to town and everybody is in a festive mood. It is the kind of situation in which rural white folk almost forgive Negroes for being colored. Something like the Christmas spirit.

A black man and his wife and children get into their Sunday-go-to-meetings, and start off for the circus, where they will pay the same price white folk pay, but will be given inferior seats reserved for colored only. They are mingling in the crowd heading down the main stem toward the Big Tent.

Whatever cares they have in the world they have left back in colored town. Then a white man, filled to the overflow with good feeling and corn whiskey, playfully pats the black man's wife on her buttocks. What the heck—he didn't mean any harm. He was smiling when he did it. Furthermore, he was drunk and cutting the fool and obviously not responsible for what he was doing.

Now this black man has two alternatives, possibly even three. He can pretend he didn't see the white man pat his wife's backside, he can pretend it was an accident, or he can die. Let's say he is a damn fool, and he knocks the white man down. In Plum Nelly, Georgia, which is any little two-by-four one-horse town in Dixie, he has signed his death warrant. Inside of fifteen minutes, Law and Order and every other source of Anglo-Saxon power will merge to put the "crazy nigger" out of his misery. The cry goes out all over the county. The headlines of the tabloids scream it. The radios and TV proclaim it:

BIG BURLY NEGRO RUNS AMUCK

He will be dead before the sun comes up. Incredible? It has happened a thousand times and more.

Notwithstanding all that has transpired in this country through the centuries, especially in the hospitable Southland down upon the Suwanee

River, I am an advocate of non-violence as a tactic in the civil-rights struggle. It is practical and pragmatic; it has worked in many instances, most notably in Montgomery, Alabama. It has, moreover, placed the burden of the Black Man's Burden squarely before the nation and the entire world. It has rallied more Americans, black and white, to the cause of racial freedom than have been rallied since the days of Reconstruction. What then is the problem?

The problem is the tendency to take such a tactic and build it into a way of life, the growing tendency to invalidate all other tactics, as if the tactic of non-violence were the only road to freedom. But the truth of the matter is there are many highways and byways and depending on the circumstances every single one must be traveled.

If non-violence is gratuitously to waive the Negro's right of self-defense, even though he never had it, somebody somewhere has lost his or her perspective. Just because we black men never had the exercisable right of self-defense, does this mean at this late hour we have to relinquish it? Must we construct an ideology around it, proclaiming to the world that we black folk have at this stage in our development permanently waived the right?

In the fight to make that magnificent document

about the rights of man, the Declaration of Independence, and the Constitution of the United States, apply equally to us, we black folk must never, tacitly or otherwise, surrender one single right guaranteed to any other American. The right of the defense of self is a basic tenet in the United States Constitution. Indeed, this right of self-defense is the most basic of human rights, recognized by all peoples everywhere. It is certainly more important to black Americans than the right to eat frankfurters seated, get a black haircut in a white barbershop, or get a night's lodging in Mrs. Murphy's flophouse, may the Good Lord rest her soul in peace. It is even more important than the right to vote. For in many places in the South the Negro can't get to the polls without the right of self-defense. This right is the essence of the law of self-preservation, which is the first law of nature.

When I was in Montgomery during the bus protest movement, I was told on more than one occasion that most Negro men had stopped riding the buses long before the boycott because they could not stand hearing their women referred to as apes, bitches, nigger whores, and other terms of Southern endearment by bus drivers. Here again the alternatives were clear. Castration, death, or tired feet. In a word, black Montgomerians did not have the right to be violent, by word or action, toward any white man, however violent he might be toward them.

Notwithstanding, the South is an armed camp. It always has been, ever since I can remember. The first time my wife, who is Brooklyn-born, went South with me in 1950, she was shocked to see so many guns in Negro homes. Almost every other person had a hunting license. Nevertheless non-violence is a sound tactic, particularly if its major consideration is the practical fact that the Southern white establishment has a much greater and more efficient fire power. They have soldiers to man the guns (almost every white civilian stays in readiness for muster), not to mention law-enforcement agencies, which include city and county police, State Troopers, and National Guardsmen. Add to these such Southern groups as the Ku Klux Klan and the White Citizens Council, and you have an awesome array of power. As Sterling Brown, a Negro poet once wrote in his memorable *Old Lem:*

> They got the judges
> They got the lawyers
> They got the jury rolls
> They got the law
>   They don't come by ones

> *They got the sheriffs*
> *They got the deputies*
>> *They don't come by twos*

> *They got the shotguns*
> *They got the rope*
>> *We get the justice*

> *In the end*
>> *And they come by tens.*

Yet non-violence has the power of moral suasion. It often makes it easier to solicit help, financial and otherwise, from many white liberals who might otherwise avoid such a cause. The tragedy is that today the American Negro has to discuss with anybody, black or white, such a fundamental question as the right of self-defense. What kind of morality is it that would deny a man, because of his color, the right to defend his person?

We black folk used to have a saying in Georgia regarding the question of white morality: "Mister Charlie will do anything he's big enough and white enough to get away with."

So, what else is new?

When non-violence evolves, as it has in this case, from a tactic into an ideology, and indeed into a way of life, it presupposes that one's opponent is a moral human being. But there is no evidence to support such a presumption. Every shred of evidence leads to the contrary.

Before leading the Negro people of Birmingham into a demonstration in that city, the Rev. Martin Luther King was reported to have said, "If blood is shed, let it be our blood!" But where is the morality that makes the white racist's blood more sacred than black children's? I cannot believe that Martin King meant these words, if indeed he ever uttered them. I can only believe that if he did he got carried away by the dramatics of the moment, the stresses and strains, the rhetoric. It has happened to other men.

The Rev. Martin King is one of the men whom I have met in this life for whom I have a very deep regard and hold in great esteem. We have been friends since 1957. Yet he loses me and many other Negroes when he calls upon us to love our abusers.

There is no dignity for me in allowing another man to spit on me with impunity. There is no dignity for him or me. There is only sickness, and it will beget an even greater sickness. It degrades me and brutalizes him. Moreover, it encourages him in his bestiality. I cannot love the murderers of the Birmingham children, the killers of Evers, Schwerner, Chaney, Goodman, and Moore. If we Negroes are so sick as to love those who practice genocide against us, we are in very bad shape indeed.

The racist murders in Birmingham and in Mississippi should have convinced us once and for all, if we still needed convincing, that we black folk must assert our right of self-defense. Who will defend the Negro if he refuses to defend himself? Certainly not the forces of law and order. They are, as often as not, the actual perpetrators of the violence. And the Federal government has indicated that it either cannot or will not defend the person of the black American.

The advocates of absolute non-violence have reckoned without the psychological needs of Black America. Let me state it plainly: there is in many Negroes a deep need to practice violence against their white tormentors. Frederick Douglass was aware of this a century ago when he called on black Americans to flock to the Union colors, even though they were unwanted, and would not receive equal pay. "There is something ennobling in the possession of arms," Douglass told his black brethren, "and we of all people in the world stand in need of their ennobling influence."

Remember how deeply we black folk loved the great Joe Louis? No one, before or after, has captured the imagination of African-Americans as he did. Each time he whipped another white man black hearts overflowed with joy. Joe was strong wine for our much-abused egos. Every fight he ever fought, we were in the ring with him. *Our* Joe, not your Old Black Joe. And every triumph he experienced, we experienced. Yes, we were finally fighting back. We were fighting back against Mister Charlie in a way we had never been allowed to fight. Joe was the embodiment of our deepest wish fulfillment. He was black manhood redeemed forevermore. He paid the ransom with his fists, violence against violence, the only language that men of violence have ever understood. He was, to black folk, the Magnificent Vicarious Experience.

I was at Yankee Stadium the night he knocked out Max Schmeling in the first round. I saw black men, strangers, embrace each other unashamedly and weep for joy. I was in Harlem afterward. I know the emotions that were unleashed that night, and on every other night when our champ demolished another enemy. In Washington, Negroes overturned streetcars and buses.

In a little town in Alabama, the Negro population gathered in a dance hall to hear another of Joe's fights. The tension built as the fight progressed, and reached an even higher point as the referee began to count over another prostrate victim. When he reached the count of ten, the people who by then had congregated in the center of the floor were in such a state they all jumped up as one and they came down with such an impact that the floor collapsed. Many were injured but this did not spoil the fight for them. They had won by another knockout, hadn't they? All of us black people. Some of the Black Bourgeoisie were embarrassed by the violence the Brown Bomber perpetrated against the King's English, but to most Negroes the important thing was the violence Joe was perpetrating against Whitey, Mister Charlie.

I saw the movie *Lydia Bailey* in downtown Manhattan and then once again in Harlem. The different reactions of the two audiences to one scene was highly indicative of this feeling. When William Marshall, tall, dark, and awesome, knocked a group of French soldiers into the harbor of Port-au-Prince, the Harlem audience burst into applause. It was entirely spontaneous. The applause was absent downtown.

Most Americans never understood why thousands of Negroes turned out in front of the Hotel Theresa on a cold rainy night to greet Castro. I was there and I saw the looks of anger and confusion on the faces of the white policemen as black voices screamed *"Viva Castro! Viva Fidel!"* It had nothing to do with Communism. I heard one black brother sum up the sentiment of most of that crowd: "Yeah, I dig Fidel the most. Any time a man kicks Whitey's ass, he's okay with me!"

Revenge? No, revenge is not the motivation. Racial hatred? No. Black chauvinism? Again, no, we are not Genêt's *Blacks,* waiting for the day we can assume the role the white man played for centuries. When white Americans witness black Americans affirming militantly their dignity and self-respect, they have nervous breakdowns and hurl charges of racial hatred. Just because I love myself, the black *me,* why do you think it means I have to hate *you,* the white American?

Actually, just the opposite is true. No man can love another unless he loves himself first. A man who does not love himself cannot love his wife or any other woman. When I despised myself, I didn't love you. I trembled in your presence. I was in awe of you. But awe and love are poles apart. At this juncture in our relationship, love is an irrelevance. Only equals can love with dignity. The slave cannot really love his master.

We black and white folk in America have to settle many things between us before the matter of love can even be discussed. What you want from me now is not love but worship, the fawning adoration of a dog for its master. But even a dog will bite his master if he kicks him. The point is, I don't, at this juncture, need to love you.

Nor do I need to not love you. If you practice violence against me, I mean to give it back to you in kind. This is the frame of mind of most black men in this republic. Maybe this will help whip some sense into your head. Maybe there is no other way than this painful, violent road to mutual love and understanding. To encourage you in your sadistic ways is not love but abject masochism, and most black folk will no longer buy it. This is why millions of Negroes have not joined the non-violent movement.

Even most of you white liberals, who should know better, back away when I affirm my right to violence in the face of violence, which can only mean that you too deny my right of self-defense. Do you not realize how long you have been killing me? Are you not aware that atrocities against black people mount up into the hundreds of thousands? For any white man to raise the question of non-violence as a moral question with a black man is merely an indication of the depth of America's great insensitivity and degradation.

Let us speak plainly. The only reason black men have not long ago resorted to violence is that white men have the more powerful weapons and the greater numbers. We don't need to beg the question of morality; the burden of proof is on America. The ethics of the slave are always superior to those of his master.

We black folk believe in the kind of non-violence that keeps everybody non-violent. We believe in non-violence in depth, the kind that stays the hand of the perpetrators of violence. For example: In a certain Tennessee county that borders on Mississippi, black folk, most of them sharecroppers, asserted their right to vote and were driven from the land that most of them had worked on all of the days of their lives. For several years they lived in tents, and of a Saturday evening white pranksters had a playful way of driving out to Tent City and shooting into it. A couple of tent dwellers were injured, including a pregnant woman and a veteran, but complaints to the proper authorities got no results. So one Saturday evening the man bit the dog. The next time the pranksters appeared for a little sport the tent dwellers returned the fire, and a young relative of the sheriff got his arm shattered. The sheriff got out there in a hurry and found a Winchester sticking out of each tent.

He hurriedly sent for John McFerren, one of the Negro leaders. "Tell them to give up them rifles, John. I can't protect them 'less'n they surrender up them rifles."

McFerren said to the sheriff: "We figured you was kind of busy, Sheriff. We thought we'd give you a helping hand and protect our own selves."

The Saturday-night shooting sprees came to an

abrupt conclusion. There was no more racial vio-lence in the county for a long time. This is the kind of non-violence that keeps everybody non-violent.

So please do not give us the example of India and Mohandas Karamchand Gandhi. The situa-tions are not similar; they could not be more dis-similar. In our country, Negroes are in the minori-ty; in his, his people were in a vast majority. The black American is outnumbered nine to one; the Indians outnumbered the British by at least a thousand to one. And in the same context Ameri-ca is a *white* country, the Mahatma's had been Indian forever. There were enough Indian bodies to literally form a wall against the imperialistic British and stop them from functioning. And fur-ther, India was not uniformly non-violent. Even as Gandhi preached non-violence, violence often-times exploded in the hinterlands.

The great fallacy of the whole non-violent ide-ology in America is that it is based on a set of circumstances and historical realities totally un-American. We black folk are captives in the land of our birth; but we are also in the land of our estrangement. The British in India were always foreigners, even though they ruled.

And lastly, the fact that we Americans are a nation of violence should give staunch advocates of non-violence pause for reflection. We have always been a nation of violence. Our, rather your, proud forefathers killed off an entire race whom they arrogantly called Indians, though they knew well enough they were not in India. And when John Fitzgerald Kennedy was assassinated little white children cheered in Dallas schools, and as at least one newspaper morbidly pointed out, in the comparatively short time of our existence as a nation we have assassinated more of our leaders than any nation in history. In classic Latin American coups, they at least put their rulers on airliners and give them a running start. We also dropped the most devastating bombs ever dropped in a military operation, and we dropped them on civilians—in Hiroshima and Nagasaki. Most colored people are convinced that those bombs were dropped there because the people we dropped them on were colored. There are a lot of colored people in this world, yet our ex-President apparently feels no deep remorse, a fact that possibly reflects the very low degree of sensitivity exhibited by most Americans toward a goodly share of the human race. It's mostly colored, you know.

I was an American soldier in the Philippines when the bombs were dropped. My outfit was preparing to form part of a task force that would have invaded the Japanese homeland. I remember the relief all of us felt when we heard the news and realized the war was nearly over, for many of us would have discolored the immaculate beaches of Japan with our patriotic blood. Yet after those first moments of rejoicing, there was a time of sober reflection.

I recall one of the men in my outfit saying in dead seriousness: "The thing they should do now is dump the rest of those fucking bombs in the middle of the Pacific, destroy the formula, then round up all the bloody scientists who know anything about that formula and blow their fucking brains out!"

Only the stars in the heavens could have kept track of the acts of violence perpetrated on the black American in his native land. If the Southern waters gave up their dead, if all that strange and bitter fruit hung from Southern trees again, what a sight for human eyes. What a retching of queasy stomachs. How long, America? How long, especially my friends of the liberal persuasion, how long, in the light of this violence against me, can you continue to speak to me of non-violence? The chasm widens steadily. Soon it will no longer be possible for me to hear you.

For your black brother *is* spoiling for a fight in affirmation of his manhood. This is the cold-blooded, Gospel truth. The more violence perpetrated against him, with pious impunity, the more he becomes convinced that this thing cannot resolve itself non-violently, that only blood will wash away the centuries of degradation. The burden is on White America to prove otherwise. But you had better get going in a hurry, for we are at the brink.

5

The Black Mystique
or
Would You Want
One of Them
to Marry
Your Daughter?

JAMES BALDWIN MADE one of the sharpest obser-
vations he has made in his short, illustrious life
one Sunday over television, when he stared long
and hard at John Kilpatrick, Southern genteel
aristocrat from old Virginia, and stated matter-of-
factly:

"You're not worried about me marrying *your*
daughter. You're worried about me marrying

your *wife's* daughter. I've been marrying your daughter ever since the days of slavery."

In the whole body of Negro-white dialogue, which has collected for over a hundred years, this bugaboo about marrying Mister Charlie's daughter is the *non sequitur* to end all *non sequiturs*. Indeed it would be ludicrous if white Americans had not made into a subjective reality what was historically an objective irrelevance. The fact of the matter is that the American Negro is the most multi-colored people on this planet, not because Old Black Joe married Miss Ann, nor did we become these many colors because Uncle Tom raped Little Eva. So let us try to put some of these myths to rest once and for all. Let us, at the very least, place things in their perspective.

During slavery old Massa put his white wife on a pedestal and threw Aunt Jemima in the Big House bed, or went down into the cabins and raped Aunt Hagar's defenseless young-uns. So that while old Missus was withering on the vine like a raisin in the sun, the kindly master was sowing black oats and making heaps of yaller chilluns. And that's how the American black race became so many colors, from coal-ebony all the way across the spectrum to blond and pinkish white. Thus we have to say, old Massa and his Caucasian heirs are the "Last of the Great Miscegenators."

Frances Anne Kimbel, a famous English actress who married a slaveholding Georgia plantation owner, describes in a letter to a friend a conversation she had had with Sophy, a slave. It was not an unusual conversation within the context of the Southern slavery system, but it serves to demonstrate this aspect of that peculiar institution:

Sophy went on to say that Isaac was her son by driver Morris [white,] who had forced her while she was in her miserable exile at Five Pound. Almost beyond my patience with this string of detestable details, I exclaimed— foolishly enough, heavens knows: "Ah! but don't you know—did nobody ever tell you that it is a sin to live with men who are not your husband?"

Alas, Elizabeth, what could the poor creature answer but what she did, seizing me at the same time vehemently by the wrist: "Oh yes, Missis, we know—we know all about dat well enough; but we do anything to get our poor flesh some rest from the whip; when he made me follow him into the bush, what use me tell him no? He has the strength to make me."*

---

* Frances Anne Kimbel, *Journal of a Residence on a Georgian Plantation*.

Or lend your ears to Mary Boykin Chestnut, a great white Southern lady, speaking of slavery as she knew it:

God forgive us, but ours is a monstrous system, a wrong and an iniquity! Like the patriarchs of old, our men live all in one house with their wives and their concubines; and the mulattoes one sees in every family partly resemble the white children. Any lady is ready to tell you who is the father of all mulatto children in everybody's household but her own. Those, she seems to think, drop from the clouds.*

The mother of my maternal grandfather was thirteen years old when my grandfather was born. Notwithstanding the fact that he was born more than a decade after slavery, kindly masters had not given up their devilish ways or their slavery-time prerogatives. Young Master, old Master's favorite son, raped my great-grandmother when she was twelve and he was at the gay-blade age of twenty-one. Needless to say, the young cut-up did not make an honest woman out of my great-grandmother. That is not the way things were done in those days. Neither is that the way things

---

* Mary Boykin Chestnut, *Diary from Dixie.*

are done in these days by the Southern gentlemen of quality.

Evolving out of this mongrelization of a proud and pure race, there grew a people who came to be designated as Negroes, mulattoes, quadroons, or octoroons. The dictionary is very helpful and enlightening on this subject. Accordingly, an octoroon is "a person having one-eighth Negro blood, the offspring of a quadroon and a white."

Do I hear you ask, "But what in the devil is a quadroon?" A quadroon is "a person who is one-fourth Negro; the offspring of a mulatto and a white." And a mulatto is "the offspring of parents of whom one is white and the other a Negro." Now let us find out what a Negro is. A Negro is "a person having more or less Negro blood." So you see, after all the rigmarole, an octoroon is a Negro, a quadroon is a Negro, a mulatto is a Negro, a Negro is a Negro is a Negro is a Negro. Any questions?

In many Southern states, one drop of black blood in your white veins makes you an American Negro. We black folk are indeed a powerful race of people. I mean we really leave our imprint on a nation.

And now it must be stated that although old Massa, or young Massa for that matter, never married the young black sapling-of-a-lass whom he had got in a family way, he very often gave preferential treatment to her and his progeny. His and Hers were often allowed to play with the master's legitimate children. The young "bucks" wore young Massa's hand-me-downs, and sometimes the young "heifers" inherited the young Missy's last year's pretty-things. They were allowed to clean old Massa's boots, and sometimes lick them in the bargain.

Thus was an aristocracy of color established which in many instances still persists. The more you resembled the folks in the Big House the better off you were. You were a "house nigger" and you came to be contemptuous of "field niggers," the toilers and the sweaters, who were mostly pure and black, just like they'd come from Mother Africa. But you were also contemptuous of yourself because you hated that part of you that wasn't like the Master Race, and deep down inside you thought of yourself and others like you as bastards, even though you were the bastards of the privileged. You looked at yourself through the eyes of the Big House people who thought of you as bastards. Notwithstanding, with your white blood, you were "better off" than the pure blacks working the fields of cotton.

Thus literary myths were also created, even by such formidable and well-meaning stalwarts as Harriet Beecher Stowe; the myth that only mulatto "niggers" were sassy and militant and hard to control because of their white blood, which naturally responded negatively to enslavement. And pure blacks were meek and docile and child-like and hard-working, though they were lazy and had to be driven, or so the scripts of the black myths read, always written by white writers. But what they failed to explain was the pure blacks of the Harriet Tubman and Nat Turner ilk, and all those other black rebellious souls.

Great Harriet Tubman, little black woman, Moses of her people, who escaped slavery via the Underground Railroad but was not satisfied with her own freedom; she couldn't sit still till the South was free. She went back South, deep down into Egypt Land nineteen times, with a price on her head, dead or alive, and she led more than three hundred slaves to freedom, a rifle always at her side. She was the greatest Underground conductor of them all; her boast: "My train never ran off the track, and I never lost a passenger."

And old Nat Turner, black and strong and mighty in his righteous anger, insurrectionist whose religion was freedom, a "religious fanatic" in the great tradition of Toussaint L'Ouverture and Gabriel Prosser, Denmark Vesey or old John Brown of Bloody Kansas.

Neither could these scripts of myths explain those black folk who staged "slowdowns" all over the old plantation South when they broke the hoes and plows and other farming implements accidentally-on-purpose.

But the hegemony of color was established and persisted. It was established by the Establishment and for the blessed Establishment. It was a part of the Great Brainwash. Every Negro was taught that the closer you were to white the better off you were in the eyes of the man, the white man that is. And the white man's eyes were the ones that mattered. It was in him the power resided. He spread the table where there were high-class crumbs for the "gitting." So the octoroon looked down upon the quadroon who looked down upon the mulatto and all looked down upon the low man on the totem pole, who was hopelessly and helplessly black and had no one to look down upon.

So "good hair" and "bad hair" and "high yaller" became a part of the language. Desperate Negro mothers massaged the noses of black babies trying to mold them into thinner and narrower shapes. The endless futile admonitions: "Don't poke out your mouth, it'll make you grow to have big ugly lips. Don't drink coffee. It'll make you black." The myths of abnegation: "Black folks study evil. A black gal sleeps with her fists balled up." I grew up in this kind of culture, steeped in self-hatred. And yet somehow our self-hatred was not as deep-seated as might be imagined. Somehow, despite the Great Brain-wash, we loved ourselves and loved each other.

I remember Madame Walker's hair straightener and I recall the aroma of burned hair and vase-line; even now my mind makes pictures of tired hands and straightening combs and bleaching creams. And for us boys the pomades, the "slickums" with which we plastered our poor heads, the stocking cap in which we slept all night long. Then Upsouth in New York and other Up-south cities the process was discovered to straight-en black men's hair. And so the "conk" came into vogue, though it did not catch every black man's fancy. It was probably at that time that many black men began to see the ridiculous lengths to which we had extended ourselves in order to resemble the Master Race.

Yes, old Massa really started something. But at this point in time and space, we are ringing down the curtain. Sure, there were Negro churches in the South even in my time where a man with a black face had better not set foot unless he was the janitor. There were Negro colleges which had quotas for those with very dark com-plexions. And in places like Charleston, South Carolina, or Washington, D.C., some of us were anti-Negro and color-conscious to a degree that bordered on sickness. But we are ringing down the curtain. Notwithstanding the formidable de-brainwashing job before us, we black folk are ringing down the curtain.

In the West Indies, even to this day, old Massa oftentimes had thirty and forty mulatto children borne by ten or twelve black women. In many of these cases, though Mister Charlie hardly ever married any of them, he oftentimes had at least one of them living with him in the Big House, and others vying for his favor. The offspring of these "happy" situations more often than not rejected their black mothers out of hand and basked in the sunshine of their benevolent great white fathers. To give the devil his due, though for the life of me I can't imagine why I should, old Massa often treated such offspring more or less as his own children. They came to make up the managerial class on the plantation and when the great white father passed on, the plantation went to his mulatto children. This progressive paternalism has created a color caste in much of the Caribbean, the lines of which are drawn far sharper than any to be found in the U.S.A. Many West Indian mulattoes even today regard themselves as "colored," and look upon black West Indians as Negroes, even "niggers," or "darkies," and obviously a lesser people.

Yet in spite of this the Establishment would

have us believe that the entire struggle between black and white in this country has its roots in the determination of the whites to hold the line and maintain the purity of the races and the sanctity of Southern womanhood, while the black man lives only for the day when he will catch Miss Anne with her restrictions down, and that all else is verbiage and hypocrisy. Civil rights—the right to vote, the right to work, the right not to be lynched, all the slogans about freedom and justice and equality—are merely part of a Black Master Plan to get the black man into the white woman's bed so he can mongrelize the races.

It is a peculiar fact that marrying Whitey's daughter is always the first line of defense set up by the Southern white man against the black, yet it appears nowhere in the bill of particulars set forth by the black man in his case against the White Establishment. Examine for days, months—years if you will—the records of the N.A.A.C.P., of C.O.R.E., the Urban League, or S.N.C.C., and you will find in none of their varied programs one single slogan about the right to marry Mister Charlie's daughter. Historically, it has always been a smoke screen set up by the White Establishment to becloud any just demand of black folk. Its over-all aim has been to maintain the *status quo,* to keep the Negro in his place, at the bottom of the economic ladder, and incidentally to keep the poor white near enough the bottom so that both of them would be shackled forever together in bondage to the Southern Way of Life. The poor white oftentimes had nothing save his vaunted whiteness to distinguish him from the black man just beneath him, and what easier ruse than to convince him that his whiteness was in jeopardy, that the black man wanted only to bed down with his white women and make the white race into a bunch of "yaller niggers"?

Thus the Black Mystique had its humble beginnings as an economic and political expediency. In order to carry out the Grand Design for Exploitation known as the Southern Way of Life, you had to deny the black man any social or sexual equality, because the alternative was to admit to the world (and to the poor white Southerner) that the Negro was not a beast but a man like any other man. But if you kept him in the animal kingdom obviously you would not be expected to invite him into your home, to break bread at your table, and to marry your darling daughter. Obviously certain inalienable rights—to vote, to hold office, to work other than as a beast of burden, to enjoy life, liberty, and the pursuit of happiness—were not endowed him by his Creator.

But a mystique is never static. In order to maintain it, you must build upon it. To the myth of the animal-like sexual obsession of the black man, you must add the myth of great sexual prowess. He is generously equipped for the sex act, like a stud horse, and equally tireless. And there is this too about mystiques; eventually everybody believes the myths, both the victims and the victimizers. The myth makers become the victims of their own propaganda. So that when Whitey, the Last of the Great Myth Makers, comes face to face with his victim, the black man, he really believes he stands before his sexual superior. He sees a phallic symbol as prodigious as the Empire State Building.

There is yet another dimension to this portrait. Is it not possible that the white man sees his own lust reflected in the black man's eyes? A guilt constructed out of centuries of playing the role of Sheik in the Great White Harem, where black men were eunuchs and black women were concubines, and though Number One wife was always white, she was merely a figurehead, a wife and mistress in name only. The black man, a eunuch no longer, looks upon all this and wonders: Has the Great White Harem made a loveless lot out of all of white America? Have Americans become a people anxious to be loved but incapable of loving?

And does it not stand to reason that this has not left the white woman disinterested? She was never a free soul in the harem; she, too, was one of the exploited. The myth about the black man's sexual prowess has undoubtedly made her more curious than she might ordinarily have been about the forbidden fruit. Is it really true? Is he really as formidable a lover as they say he is?

Is it any wonder that the white man lives with a built-in nightmare of his own construction? He is afraid of retribution—from both sides. Having historically been the exploiter of both women and black folk, economically, socially, psychologically, and sexually, the two might even band together against him. This may explain why the white woman seems to have less trouble than the white man in shedding her racial prejudices. Generalizations are dangerous, but even among young liberals and progressives the white male appears to have a much harder struggle.

I have studied young folk gathered in an office to get out a mailing for a civil-rights demonstration. More often than not, the white girls mingle easily and with little or no self-consciousness. They will very usually put their heads and shoulders together with the black youth, intent on getting the job done. Whereas you will often notice young white boys, equally as dedicated and sincere, are much more self-conscious. Oftentimes, unknowingly, they are watching for the interplay, real or imagined, between Missy and young black

Joe. It is the nature of the sickness of this society. No soul is left unscathed.

The question: "How would you like one of them to marry your daughter?" is, of course, a gratuitous comment on every white woman in this nation. It is also very revealing as to the state of mind of most of the white American males. How came you to this abyss of insecurity, this ignobility, whereby you shamelessly imply that all of your darling daughters are forever red in the face and panting for breath and straining at the leash, looking toward that morning when they are free, at which time they will kick over the traces and go for all the prizes, that day when the legal and conventional fences are down, and they will all dash lickety-split to leap into the black man's bed. You have allowed your anxieties to run away with your imagination.

After all, marriage is a contract entered into freely by both parties. That means that nobody can marry your daughter unless your daughter wills it. And by the same token, your daughter cannot marry a single one of Uncle Tom's grandsons unless the grandson wills it. You and I, in the final analysis, do not, cannot, and should not have a damn thing to say about it.

I remember the summer when I was sixteen years old and worked at a hotel in my home town of Macon. Ask any black bellhop. We black kids were scared to death most of the time. You were sixteen and they rang for room service in Suite 715. You knew that room service meant any service the traffic would bear, so when you reached the door you hesitated, sometimes made the Sign of the Cross (it was not unlike moving out onto the Hollywood Freeway), swallowed hard, and knocked, knowing that once that door opened anything could happen.

The door finally swings back and there stands the white woman eternally aimed at your poor black head like a loaded rifle. She may be in varied degrees of dishabille, even like Lady Godiva, sometimes, without her horse, standing there as if you do not exist as a man, desexing you with her eyes, though you suspect at the same time that she may covet you. So you stand there, sixteen years old, feeling your age and knowing your place, tongue-tied and perspiring, hating this white woman and yet somehow feeling a strange kind of pity for her. Then the gruff voice from the other room:

"Tell the nigger to bring the stuff in here, Lucy Belle."

But before you could get yourself together, he comes stumbling naked toward the door. "Hey, boy, what you looking at a white woman like that for?"

You hate yourself for saying what you have to say. "I'm not looking at anybody, sir. No, sir!"

"You calling me a liar, boy?"

"No, sir! I just mean you were mistaken!"

You turn to go. The hell with the tip.

"Where you going, boy? Bring that stuff on into the bedroom."

You're in the bedroom now. "Nigger, ever since you been in this suite you ain't been able to keep your eyes offa Miss Lucy Belle."

"No, sir. You are mistaken, sir."

"What's the matter? You think she ugly?"

"No, sir!"

"I bet you got a great big tool all right. What you reckon, Lucy Belle?"

"Leave the boy alone, George Henry."

There were two or three incidents like that per week, with variations, but somehow you got through the summer with your manhood and your sanity intact. When I remember that summer, and think of all the black men who have been lynched, legally and otherwise—the Scottsboro Boys, the Martinsville Seven, Willie McGee, and Emmett Till—I am certain that some white women must shudder at the way they have let themselves be used against the black man. They have been the justification for every evil ever perpetrated in the name of Southern Womanhood. White women must know they have been used, and abused, historically. They still have very few rights that a white man must respect. White women have prerogatives of inferiority and they have learned to live with them in this the white man's world. Some even look upon them as privileges.

The feminine mystique is as tricky as the black mystique, and after all is said and done the white woman settles, too, for the Master's leavings. She eats much higher on the hog than black folk, but the choicest morsels are still left for old Massa.

There was a time when white and black women declared a common cause. Great abolitionist Sojourner Truth was in the fight for women's rights. Many of those in the Suffragette and Women's Rights movement were also rabid abolitionists; women like Ernestine Rose and many others. Frederick Douglass, the great abolitionist and ex-slave, also made common cause with the struggle for women's rights. He saw no contradiction. And there was none.

Is it any wonder that old Massa lives with a growing horror that worms turn sometimes, that the victims might compare notes again, as has happened throughout history; that one day the victims, black and white, might join forces? A guilty conscience does an inordinate amount of worrying. But this is not the kind of conscience that rids itself of guilt and worrying by righting wrongs. It will be up to the victims to clear the victimizers' consciences by righting the wrongs of centuries and changing the emphases of this society. This is the only way wrongs are righted. It was ever thus.

6

Black Man's Burden

THE NEGRO PROBLEM and the White Man's Burden are historical misnomers. The Problem never was "Negro." The Problem is, and ever was, Caucasian, Anglo-Saxon, European, white. And today, at this very moment, the problem facing most of the races of mankind is: "What are we going to do about these white folk? How are we going to get them off our backs; how can we undo their centuries of deliberate dehumanization? And having liberated ourselves from them—politically, economically, socially, psychologically, culturally —how are we going to integrate them into our New World of Humanity where racial prejudice will be obsolete and the whiteness of their skin will not be held against them, though neither will it afford them any special privileges? How are we going to teach them the meaning of some of the phrases they themselves claim to have invented but never practiced so far as we were concerned—democracy, human dignity, and the brotherhood of man?" This is the enormous Black Man's Burden today. There never was a White Man's Burden within this context unless it was his guilty conscience, assuming that he had a conscience where black men were concerned.

The Black Man's Burden, simply stated, was slavery and colonialism.

Once upon a time, not too many centuries ago (in the context of the infinity of time and space), stingy-mouthed men of little pigmentation, who dwelt in midget-sized kingdcms of Europe, embarked on a bloody venture of empire. American aborigines dubbed them "palefaces," a far more accurate designation than the one they chose for themselves. They preferred to look upon themselves as white men. Now one of the first important things these palefaced ones did was to discover America. A man named Christopher Columbus got the credit for it, though obviously he did not discover America since there were already people there when he arrived. But you did not exist until the great palefaced ones discovered you; you just waited in a kind of limbo. You just existed on some exotic piece of real estate in that vast continuing "jungle" that stretched from America to Africa to Asia to the islands of the mighty oceans, a noble savage waiting to be discovered, so you could be civilized, Christianized, and/or annihilated. You had alternatives, you see.

The "Paleface" came from many and varied tribes, who, not very long before (again in the context of the millions of years of time and space), had lived in holes in the earth and had waged internecine wars and had worn no clothes save the skin of an animal which was thrown over the shoulders and fastened at the breast by a thorn or a sharp-pointed stick. A few centuries later, this same barbaric people had become the Master Race.

Having discovered America, the palefaced ones brought black men there from the continent of Africa, brought them across the Atlantic in the holds of ships stacked together like cordwood, men, women, and children. Thousands of African villages were depopulated. Some still are to this very day. Peaceful villages were devastated. Chiefs and kings were corrupted, and many of the indigenes, who worked hand in glove with the "nigger catchers," were in their own turn made captives. More than sixty million Africans lost their lives in transit, for most of the ships were floating death traps, ridden with plague and other epidemics. The unwilling passengers ate, moved their bowels, vomited, urinated, slept in their own defecation, sickened and died in their cramped allotted space. If they were lucky, after England outlawed slavery, a British ship might spot the slave ship and then the captain would throw the whole load overboard, chained to one another, thus sparing them the slow death of the Middle Passage, or the even slower death that awaited them at the journey's end.

Most of the unfortunate survivors were sold into slavery in America, that haven for all men who cherished freedom, perhaps the cruelest irony in history. Sweet Land of Liberty, the brave New World, this New Hope for all mankind, became the stage upon which was enacted the most inhuman drama in the entire history of man's brutality to man. By comparison, the Nazi bestiality seems almost an exercise in tiddlywinks. The reason the rest of the civilized world did not rise up in protest was that the victims were pagans, a savage race deemed fortunate to be brought to America, under whatever conditions, where they could be civilized and Christianized. But the blacks did not believe in their good fortune. Many leaped into the sea en masse; others mutinied; and every known method of committing suicide was attempted. The blacks were truly an ungrateful lot.

Having invented the Negro to justify slavery, the Negro invention was used as an apologia for the colonialization of three-quarters of the world's people, in Asia, Africa, and the Islands. Thus there evolved but two kinds of people on this earth—men and non-men, white folk and "niggers," Christians and heathens, masters and slaves. It is a peculiar thing that Western men showed such shock at Der Führer's theory of the Master Race when for centuries they had taken this theory for granted in relation to the darker races of the world.

But now we have reached a moment when time is catching up with history. Throughout most of the earth Time and History and Folk have entered into a conspiracy to put an end to the domination of the palefaced ones. There was a time not too far past, when people of Africa looked upon Americans of African descent as especially fortunate people, who would one day, from their superior positions, help their less fortunate brothers and sisters to liberate Mother Africa. And now it has come to pass that black Americana may be the last people on earth to achieve freedom and human dignity. It is another irony of history that the place that gave birth to the Black Man's Burden may be the very last place where the black man will lay that burden down.

"Outside Africa," I thought, "the old world of the West is dying." Inside Africa, a New World is a-borning. During my first trip to that ageless continent, we followed the mighty Niger River hundreds and hundreds of miles all the way to the ancient city of Timbuktu, which had a university (Sankore) centuries before the first European landed in America. We traveled deep into the Niger Delta to old Calibar and Port Harcourt and Bonny in the Bight of Benin, where the mangroves seem to be creeping farther and farther out into the ocean, bringing the continent along with them. I visited ten African countries—villages, farms, the vast and endless countryside, teeming cities, the hot and barren desert. In Nigeria, Ghana, Upper Volta, Togo, Dahomey, Senegal, Mali, Guinea, Sierra Leone, Niger, Liberia, everywhere I got the firm impression that Africa was giving birth to a brand-new world at the very moment that the Western world was dying, though grandiosely, amid pretty slogans of Free Worlds and NATO's, A&P's and SEATO's, New Frontiers and Warsaw Pacts, and H-bombs and earth satellites. The Old World of the West was dying over the length and breadth of this death-driven earth.

I had not gone to Africa in search of Western values as some of my friends have done. I had not wanted to find New York in Lagos, Accra, or Ouagadougou. I had had enough of the West for a time. Yes, the West was sick as I saw it, and I was sick of the West. The West was using a New Look to cure cancer. The patient needed basic surgery, but instead went daily to Madison Avenue to have his or her face lifted.

Sure, I know. It is hard for a people to admit to themselves that they are a part of a dying civilization. They are sitting on top of the world, fat and well-appointed, overfed, the picture of disgustingly good health. "I've got the world in a jug and the stopper in my hand. How could I be dying? I'm the richest guy who ever lived. I'm free and white and twenty-one. How could I be in a decline? People are just jealous of me."

It must have been no easier for the Romans, the Greeks, the Egyptians, or the Sodomites to smell of the stench of their own decadence.

When we speak of the West in this dialogue we mean the western as well as the eastern part of Western civilization. The Cold War division of the world into Eastern and Western camps is but another example of the exaggerated self-importance with which the European looks upon

himself. What he really means is Eastern and
Western white people. We also include in the
"West," arbitrarily for our purpose, New Zea-
land and Australia and the Republic of South
Africa.

One has only to look at the map of the world
as it was in 1945 and compare it with a map of
today to get an idea of the decline of Western
power and influence. There was a time when En-
glishmen could rightly boast that the sun never set
on the British Empire and France ruled great
hunks of Africa and Asia. Colored peoples
throughout the world were dominated by the palefaces. Did Sir Winston Churchill have prescience
when he proclaimed with forced bravado that he
had not taken over the reins of Her Majesty's
Government to preside over the dissolvement of
the British Empire?

That this civilization is at death's door, some
Western sages will admit, and this is disquieting
enough. But the suspicion, indeed the growing evidence that the rest of the world will not voluntari-
ly lie down and die along with the West must
be nothing short of terrifying to most of the Western wise men. And here is the rub: The deadly
germ killing the West is not necessarily fatal to
the other three-quarters of the earth's people.
They will fight off the germ, Genêt and his avant-
garde notwithstanding, and black and brown men

will survive to write the West's obituary. Can you imagine the slave master living with the fear that his liberated slaves will preach his funeral oration? So Western man lives with a built-in nightmare that the disinherited will soon inherit the earth and rewrite the history of the last five hundred years, so that "niggers" will be vindicated from Birmingham to Johannesburg, another way of saying that mankind no matter his color will at long last be vindicated. Alan Albert was right when he wrote in *Presence Africaine* that one of the cruelest things Western man had done was to "build a fence between man and man." It should be obvious that Western man meant to fence three-quarters of mankind out but all he has notably succeeded in doing is to fence himself in. In the middle of the twentieth century the West finds itself suddenly in a self-constructed isolation ward. The hope of America, indeed its sole salvation, is that the Freedom Movement will tear the fences down and bring this country into the family of mankind. This, too, is a part of the Black Man's Burden.

The people of this nation must make a grave decision: whether to die along with the rest of the aging West or to live in freedom and dignity with this New World a-borning. Put the question another way: "Is America too young to die of old age?" Young Australia has to answer similar questions. "Are we Australians ready and willing to live in equality with the races of mankind?" There is Australia, a vast continent with a smaller population than the city of New York; instead of reaching out her hands to most of mankind residing on her doorsteps, she stares ten thousand miles away toward white men in a dying Western World. The two-thirds of humanity in her front yard are invisible to her. It seems to me that young Israel must wipe the West out of her eyes and turn them toward the New World, which she must be a part of if she is to live in peace and freely prosper, the New World which is neither East nor West, as we understand the Cold War terms, but somewhere in between where the twain is meeting, Rudyard Kipling notwithstanding.

Everywhere I went in Africa I talked with dignified black men of state, ministers of commerce and labor and health, ministers of information, farmers, mechanics, road-builders, civil servants, market women, presidents, and prime ministers. And I thought of the black students back in my own country baring their heads to policemen's nightsticks and their souls to the scorn of their white countrymen for the privilege of eating a hamburger in some two-bit restaurant. I thought of my great friend Martin Luther King; I thought of my friend Daisy Bates; I thought of Abernathy and Rosa Parks and Shuttleworth and Galamison, men and women of inexhaustible dignity bending their knees in prayer and turning the other cheek in order to win such taken-for-granted human rights as the right to vote and go to school and ride in the front of a Southern bus. I thought how low our sights still have to be in my home-land of the brave and free, where some black men drive big Cadillacs and own beautiful homes with swimming pools, yet none has manhood and dignity which he can assert any time, any place. I thought, my country is not ready for the Epoch of the colored peoples.

Everywhere I went people called me brother ... "Welcome, American brother." It was a good feeling for me, to be in Africa. To walk in a land for the first time in your entire life know-ing within yourself that your color would not be held against you. No black man ever knows this in America.

No European-American can ever know the pre-cise feelings I experienced in Africa. Perhaps the Jew when he sets foot in Israel, but I doubt it. No people in recorded history has known an expe-rience similar to the African-American. In slavery our link with our past was deliberately and sys-tematically destroyed, tribes and families sepa-rated, husbands cut off from their wives, mothers cut off from their suckling babes, our voices muted as they substituted a strange tongue for the one our mothers had given us. They taught us to despise the land from whence we came, even as they despised us in the land in which we found ourselves. And we seldom found ourselves.

In Africa one feels profoundly (against one's Western skepticism) that societies are being constructed, oriented to people rather than to things. Things are not the goal in life, but the means of achieving the pursuit of happiness. One got the feeling, a feeling one wants desperately to believe, that a new dialogue for mankind is evolving in this New World. Time and again I heard variations of that same continuous theme: "We are building a civilization oriented to man. This has been true of us historically. Our governments, our religions, our traditions, our gods are all people-oriented. You people of the West are worshipers of things. You are primarily a gadget civilization. You even think to impress us by which of you can make the biggest bomb to cause the most destruction, or which of you will make the first trip to the moon. Yet you have not figured out how to live with each other here on earth. You of the West have made great progress in technology, and we must learn from you this technology, but we will give to the world our own dialogue in human values." All over Africa I looked and listened, with a heart filled with hope and un-warped by Western disillusionment and cynicism. Did mankind dare to hope again? Could there be a body of ethics other than those four great rules of the West:

> Money talks.
> Everybody has a price.
> Might makes right.
> Do others before they can do you.

"The half ain't never been told," my grand-mother used to say. I've always wanted to believe this more than anything else. If everything has already been said, let us all go to the cemetery and give ourselves up and pull the earth in after us.

Night and day along the highways of West Africa it is a common sight to see automobiles or trucks pull up alongside another stalled vehicle and men get out and gather to help until they get the crippled vehicle repaired again, or at least enough so they can make it to the nearest town. About a day and a night out of Timbuktu our mighty Land Rover bogged down axle-deep in mud forty miles south of Hombouri. A few of the indigenous population appeared from no-where and tried to help us dig our way out but we only succeeded in digging ourselves a deeper and deeper grave.

This went on from 11 A.M. till midnight. I recall watching three naked children playing in a mud puddle at the side of the road. I remember their hairdo, one long patch down the middle of their heads from front to back. The temperature was well above one hundred degrees. I took off my shoes and put my feet in the water only to withdraw them instantly because of the scalding heat. I watched the children at play in all their unclothed innocence and was moved deeply by their naked poverty. They had nothing, and then suddenly I realized that they had everything. They had their country. They had human dignity. My children back in the States had far more creature comforts but they had never had a country, they were forever aliens in their own, their native land. One of those naked boys might one day be the President of the République du Mali. There was no position in their country to which they could not one day aspire. My heart filled up and overflowed. I wanted to put my arms around them and tell them that the world was theirs in a way it had never been before. At that moment they were the most beautiful children who ever existed in all the centuries of mankind's sojourn on this lonesome planet. They were the future. They were the proof that man could have a future. I thought once more of my own children and incorrigible optimist that I am I knew realistically that without fundamental changes in their own country they could never achieve the freedom of spirit and self-confidence that these naked black kids possessed. Baked black beneath a semi-desert sun, they knew their beauty without question, saw it reflected in the puddles of water and took their dignity for granted because they lived in a country where they were in style. They were the country. They lived in a land where their color was never held against them. Their color was the land and the land was their color.

I remembered what Dorothy Dandridge had told me when she returned from Europe after having worked in a film with men from Senegal. "I have brand-new values for what is beautiful, John. Those Senegalese men with their tribal scars had a look in their eyes you do not find in the eyes of American Negroes. In all their majestic blackness, they knew who they were and they were proud of who they were. It was an experience I shall never forget."

I knew what she meant. I knew the hangdog look that even the most militant among us often carry around. I know the quick laughter, often to hide the pain and anguish gnawing away at our insides. And mostly because we had to contribute to our own castration. It was expected of us. It was traditional. It was the American Way of Life. We had to give that happy-go-lucky appearance because "that's why darkies were born," according to the script. Let the black man have humility, that greatest of all virtues residing in the soul and bosom of every black man, and let him not deny it. Every American boy-child born of a black woman who lives to reach the age of manhood has done a softshoe routine for Mister Charlie at least one little old time. It is one of the vestiges of slavery. Psychologically old Massa couldn't live without his grinning, humble darkies. Most white folk aren't ready yet for the black man who tells it like it is.

No other vehicle passed our way all that day and far into the night. It was the rainy season, and Malians had sense enough to stay at home. About midnight two sets of headlights appeared on the black horizon coming toward us. When the truck reached us they stopped, and the men jumped down and had us out of our predicament within half an hour. One of the men, a Tuareg, told us that it was against the law in Mali to pass another vehicle in trouble on the road. I thought to myself, "In America if you saw a car stalled at night by the side of the road and somebody trying to wave you down, the first thing that would cross your mind would be that somebody was trying to rob you. And nine times out of ten, somebody *would* be trying to rob you!"

Was it possible in this the mid-twentieth-century world for Africa and Asia to accept the techniques of the West without absorbing Western values in the process? Could one realistically separate form from content, accepting one while rejecting the other? Or are they one and indivisible?

It is time for Americans, and particularly Negro Americans, to understand that so long as this nation's *raison d'être* is "free enterprise" rather than "free people" there will be the Haves and the Have-Nots, poverty in the midst of debaucheries of wealth, as newspaper headlines announce increasing unemployment while reporting Long Island matrons being burglarized of a quarter of a million dollars' worth of jewelry. So long as a society evaluates itself on the basis of how many things it can produce and at how great a profit rather than how many citizens can achieve humanity, the White Problem and the Black Man's Burden will be forever with us. In almost every independent country in Africa, people are building what they call Pan-African Socialism, a socialism not of foreign import but based on their own indigenous frame of reference. If socialism is a dirty word to many of my countrymen, why call it socialism? If it conjures up Russian bogeymen, forget it. Call it "Africanism," or "true democracy," if the words taste better in your mouth.

We in America need to reconstruct our society so that people take precedence over property, and all men—white, black, brown, yellow—are masters, and only things are slaves.

I believe it is time for Negro leaders to evaluate all the philosophies of man, unmindful of the American Establishment's dos and don'ts. We should have no illusions about any establishment anywhere, past or present. Its function is to keep itself in business, to perpetuate the *status quo*. It only gives ground when it cannot help itself. The *status quo* is the curse of black existence and always has been. Negroes, who can only profit from change, are ever in a state of undeclared war against the *status quo*.

And if we let the Establishment choose the ball park for this conflict, and set all the ground rules, we can never win the World Series. And to win the World is precisely what this game is all about. Nothing short of winning the whole terrifying beautiful world.

One of the ground rules that the Establishment has laid down hard and fast is the fiction that the Negro question is a family affair; that it may not be taken by Negroes into the world arena because we might embarrass our benevolent Great White Father. If there is one thing we black folk should know by now it's that the American people are not one big happy family. We never have been. We are not even one big unhappy family. And many of the paltry concessions made us by the Establishment were due to world opinion, precisely to the Cold War, and even more precisely to the emerging countries of Africa and Asia.

To the extent that the Negro does not employ world opinion as a lever, to that same extent will the Establishment understand that the Negro is not really serious about his freedom. He is not yet angry enough. He is like a woman whose husband beats her nightly, but she does not cry out because she doesn't want the neighbors to know. She's afraid of scandalizing the family. She almost deserves to be beaten. The marriage of the sadist to the masochist is perversion pure and simple. Unrequited love is a sick bit in any context.

Yes, history is with the black American, but time is on the side of him who makes the most of it. Shakespeare was right:

> *There is a tide in the affairs of men*
> *Which taken at the flood,*
> *Leads on to fortune;*
> *Omitted, all the voyages of their life*
> *Is bound in shallows and in miseries.*

On such a full sea are we now afloat;
And we must take the current
When it serves,
*Or lose our ventures.**

The tides of freedom are lashing against the beachheads from Montgomery to Johannesburg. And we must take the current while it serves or lose our ventures.

The enemy is formidable, clever, tricky, strongly entrenched. We will have casualties. Freedom is not easily won. We will lose some of our generals and captains in this war. Some will fall in combat; some will go over to the other side. Our enemy is fantastically rich and super-affluent with those assets with which lieutenants and colonels are sometimes bribed too easily. Money, power, prestige, honor, he has all of these to burn. And our captains are only human, after all. All of our tactics will not achieve their objectives. Some strategies will backfire. Some battles will be lost. The war is the thing.

For example: when men look back upon these times, they may well render the verdict that integration was merely a detour along the road to freedom. It may very well be that "integration" was a question of putting the cart before the

---

* *Julius Caesar* by William Shakespeare.

horse. Before people are free to integrate, they must first be "free." Slaves cannot integrate with their masters. They must first be unshackled. Nor can a non-citizen integrate into a Citizen's Republic. He must first achieve citizenship. There is a basic difference between desegregation and integration, though there is a strong tendency to equate the two. Desegregation must be achieved before integration can be seriously considered. A government can desegregate its institutions; only the people themselves can integrate.

I may not want to eat a frankfurter in that two-by-four "Greasy Spoon" in Philadelphia, Mississippi, but I must have the right to do so. My son, Chuck, could not care less about marrying your daughter, but so long as there is a law against it, neither of them have freedom.

I remember a story about the first day after the buses were liberated in Montgomery. The Supreme Court had rendered its decision, and the buses were rolling again with Negroes seated in the front as big as life. All except one elderly Negro woman seated on the very back seat.

"Old woman, don't you know what the walking and praying and sacrificing for the past year was all about?" a young Negro said to her indignantly. "You're going against everything we struggled for."

The old lady stared up at him and said, *"Son,*

don't *you* know that since the Supreme Court in Washington done spoke I can sit *anywhere in this damn bus that suits my disposition?*"

Who possesses a profounder understanding of freedom and integration? The young man or the old woman?

We black folk must face our slave history and free ourselves of it and of the Great American Brainwash, which has left too many of us with a slave psychology. Our very souls have been scarred, deeply scarred, by slavery and a hundred years of segregation. Some black folk wept bitter tears for the nuns in the Congo but could find no tears to shed for Medgar Evers or the children of Birmingham. Some of us have placed the same values on our lives that most white men have.

The thing that unites all black Americans is not our aspiration to integrate into this society, or to separate from it, but our undivided determination to be free men and women in this American society. And this determination must be strong enough to unite all our leaders in winning the Great War, even though they squabble over the tactics of any particular battle. The spectacle of Whitney Young and Roy Wilkins and Dorothy Height and John Lewis and Elijah Mohammed and Martin King and Malcolm X, were he alive, seated in a united council would undoubtedly shake this nation to its very foundations. Let us

be clear on one thing. One of the reasons that
Martin Luther King has become influential with
the Establishment is because it sees the Black Na-
tionalists and Robert Williams in the wings. The
alternatives to the Rev. Martin King scare the
hell out of the power structure. This is as it
should be. Each leader serves a particular function in the movement, possesses his own integrity
and validity. No single leader has any monopoly
on integrity, or the ear of the Negro masses.

I believe it is a profound fallacy for Negroes
to think of themselves as second-class citizens.
You are either a citizen or you are not a citizen.
You are either free or you are a slave. A woman
is either pregnant or not pregnant. There is no
such thing as a half-pregnant woman or a second-
class pregnancy.

Another fallacy in the black man's perpetual
dialogue with the American people is his contin-
ual labeling of every anti-Negro attitude un-American. But the anti-Negro prototype had its beginnings in America. Where else can one find such
institutions as the Ku Klux Klan or the White
Citizens Council? They are as American as the
Coney Island hot dog and to pretend otherwise
is to engage in the idleness of wishful thinking,
a pastime that is harmless enough, but one that
never brought about a revolution. The American
reality as differentiated from the Dream and the

Promise is, and has always been, anti-Negro. The task of those of us who love this country is to change the reality, not pretend it never existed.

Notwithstanding, we black folk *are* Americans, and many of us believe our solution lies in and with America. We have been sowers here for centuries and we are determined to be reapers. But just as many of us believe the ultimate solution for the Negro is in America, we are even more firmly convinced that the ultimate salvation of America is in the Negro. This image of reality my country has thus far refused to face.

Yes, I believe profoundly that if America is not to die along with the rest of the aging Western world she must experience a new birth of freedom, and it is her black son who can help give her this.

Can you imagine what a jet-stream of creative energy will be released upon our land when twenty million black Americans become really free at last, which will mean that the whole nation will be free for the very first time in its history? Can you imagine the lift it will give our country, spiritually, creatively, economically, psychologically, when all the dikes are opened? Look at the American institutions where the restrictions have been lifted—for example, athletics. How would America fare in the Olympics without her black athletes? And the poor white Southerner will have everything to gain on that great-getting-up-morning and nothing to lose, save his "whiteness," the loss of which will be a blessing in disguise. It will mean that the time spent (which is considerable) keeping the Negro in his place may be spent for more useful and creative purposes. Far too much of the poor white Southerner's time and energy are now spent watching the back of the bus, seeing that the Negro stays back there. It will also mean that the poor white man and his black brother will be able to come together and demand a higher standard of living for everybody. I believe furthermore that the American Negro can be the bridge between the West and Africa-Asia. We black Americans can serve as a bridge to mutual understanding. The one thing we black Americans have in common with the other colored peoples of the world is that we have all felt the cruel and ruthless heel of white supremacy. We have all been "niggerized" on one level or another. And all of us are determined to "deniggerize" the earth. To rid the world of "niggers" is the Black Man's Burden; human reconstruction is the grand objective.

We black folk cannot turn back because there is nothing behind us and everything ahead of us. Too long white men have spoken for us and the result has been paternalism, overt or subtle. It is time now for the slave to chart the course to liberate the nation. Sure, we need white allies. We welcome you into our ranks. Millions of you.

Come all you who labor for your bread, you radicals and liberals and intellectuals, you artists who would change the world, you educators, who would *really* educate, you preachers, priests, and rabbis, you Democrats and Republicans, you humanists, you winter patriots who love your country. Come and go with us. Man has just begun to live. Hurry! We black folk cannot wait another moment. The tide is with us. The black commander beckons. We must put our boats to sea.

Git on board, little chillun. Git on board.

Now you and your family can take
"a guided tour to a richer life"*

How to Enjoy This Moment

by Samuel M. Silver

It is astonishing how many people have yet to discover that if you want to be happy . . . *you need only try.*

You can master the art of happiness, says Rabbi Samuel M. Silver. He shows you *how,* step by step, in over thirty *practical* chapters in HOW TO ENJOY THIS MOMENT.

Praise from outstanding leaders for HOW TO ENJOY THIS MOMENT

"It shines like a small and steady light . . . on the happiness that can be yours, if only you want to look for it . . ."
Richard Cardinal Cushing, Archbishop of Boston

"About every generation there is a first-class book on Happiness. Dr. Silver's is the best one yet."
Dr. Frederick C. Grant, Professor Emeritus, Union Theological Seminary

"It could well serve as a text for a course in the art of happiness."
Rabbi Mordecai M. Kaplan, Professor Emeritus, Jewish Theological Seminary

"(It) goes far beyond its title . . . tells us how to enjoy this moment, but more important, how to get the most out of life."
Abraham Ribicoff, United States Senator

*". . . here is a guided tour to a richer life . . ."
Sam Levenson, Author, *Everything But Money*

Read it for 10 days FREE

You will find hundreds of guidelines to a richer life . . . any one of which may be the key to happiness for you and your loved ones.

HOW TO ENJOY THIS MOMENT is available at all bookstores—or mail the coupon below and we will rush you a copy. If you don't find the book completely satisfactory, return it within ten days and owe nothing. Otherwise, we will bill you only $4.95 plus a few cents postage, as payment in full.

Trident Press, Dept. TP-3
630 Fifth Avenue, New York, N.Y. 10020

Please rush me a copy of HOW TO ENJOY THIS MOMENT to read for 10 days free. Within 10 days I will either return the book and owe nothing, or keep it and be billed $4.95, plus a few cents for shipping.

NAME ....

ADDRESS ....

CITY ....

STATE .... ZIP......................

SAVE! Enclose payment with order and we will pay shipping charges. Same 10-day refund privileges guaranteed. (Please add sales tax where applicable.)

75360

HOW
IT
WORKS

**From color camera
to computer**

1,071
two-color
drawings

**Easy-to-understand
explanations**

HOW IS color television transmitted? (See page 166 of THE WAY THINGS WORK.) How does a helicopter fly? (See page 560.) How does "dry cleaning" clean? (See page 407.)

THE WAY THINGS WORK is a lucid encyclopedia of technology, an endlessly fascinating anthology of descriptions and diagrams that unravel the mystery of common mechanisms and today's technological marvels. It's a book to delight everyone intrigued with the way things work.

We invite you to mail the coupon below. A copy of THE WAY THINGS WORK will be sent to you at once. If at the end of ten days you do not feel that this book is one you will treasure, you may return it and owe nothing. Otherwise, we will bill you $8.95, plus postage and handling. At all bookstores, or write to Simon & Schuster, Inc., Dept. W-3, 630 Fifth Ave., New York, N.Y. 10020.

SIMON & SCHUSTER, Inc., Dept. W-3
630 Fifth Ave., New York, N.Y. 10020

Please send me .... copies of THE WAY THINGS WORK. If after examining it for 10 days, I am not completely delighted, I may return the book and owe nothing. Otherwise, you will bill me for $8.95 plus mailing costs.

Name ....

Address ....

City........................... State............... Zip..........

☐ **SAVE!** Enclose $8.95 now and we pay postage. Same 10-day privilege with full refund guaranteed. (Please add applicable sales tax.)

75360

Protect yourself and your family!

Don't be one of the "taken"!

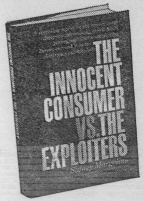

BUYER, BEWARE. Each time you walk into a store, call a serviceman, or sign a contract, you run the risk of being "taken." And not just by fly-by-night operators either. Some of the best-known and respected companies in the country lend their names to unscrupulous practices.

● Now, Sidney Margolius, leading consumer authority and an expert in financial management, shows you how to avoid being "tricked" by shady operators and operations. In his book, *The Innocent Consumer vs. The Exploiters,* you'll discover:

● How you can save up to 90 per cent on your drug bills without changing stores. (See page 195)

● The simple "instant" process that lets you calculate the real interest on a loan. (See page 37)

● Why your department store is so anxious to open a revolving charge account for you. (See page 55)

● That you are buying "balloon bread" without realizing it, fruit drinks that are 90 to 97 per cent water, and pre-sweetened cereals that are 45 per cent sugar (at $1.07 a pound.) (See page 115)

● More than an exposé, *The Innocent Consumer vs. The Exploiters* will give you the protection you need every time you open the door to a salesman. Once you've read this book, you won't be tricked—as so many have—into paying more than $400 for a TV set worth $150 which has false guarantees. And you certainly won't be one of the thousands who have their salaries garnisheed every year without even being notified.

75360

10-Day Free Trial

With all these pitfalls, one sure way to get your money's worth when you buy anything would be to bring along a lawyer, an engineer and a man from the Food and Drug Administration. Much simpler, however, is to go to your bookstore *or* fill out the coupon at right to get your copy of Sidney Margolius' revealing and helpful *The Innocent Consumer vs. The Exploiters.* If you do not believe that this book will save you many times its cost, you may return it within ten days for a full refund.

Trident Press, Dept. TP-1
630 Fifth Avenue
New York, N.Y. 10020

Please send me at once a copy of THE INNOCENT CONSUMER VS. THE EXPLOITERS. If I do not feel that this book will save me many times its cost, I may return it within ten days and owe nothing. Otherwise, you will bill me only $4.95, plus a small mailing charge.

Name _____

Address _____

City _____ State _____ Zip _____

☐ SAVE POSTAGE. Check here if you enclose check or money order for $4.95 as payment in full —then we pay postage. Same 10-day trial privilege with full refund guarantee holds. (Please add sales tax where applicable.)

Today they're playing word games.
Before he's five, he can be reading 150 words a minute.

HOW TO GIVE YOUR CHILD A SUPERIOR MIND

A remarkable new book tells how you, yourself—at home—with no special training can actually add as much as thirty points to your child's effective I.Q....how you can help him move ahead quickly in school and enable him to be more successful in an education-conscious world.

Best of all, your child can achieve this early success without being pushed and without interference with a happy, normal, well-adjusted childhood.

GIVE YOUR CHILD A SUPERIOR MIND provides a planned program of home instruction that any parent can start using immediately. *You will learn:*

1. How to awaken your child's inborn desire to learn.
2. How to teach your child to read.
3. How to help your child streak ahead in math.
4. How to give your child the power of abstract reasoning.
5. How to increase your child's effective I.Q.

At all bookstores, or mail coupon today.➤

MAIL TODAY FOR 30 DAYS' FREE EXAMINATION

SIMON & SCHUSTER, Inc., Dept. 5
630 Fifth Avenue, New York, N.Y. 10020

Please send me a copy of the new book GIVE YOUR CHILD A SUPERIOR MIND. If I am not convinced that it can show me how to increase my child's intelligence and potential for success, I may return it within 30 days and owe nothing. Otherwise I will send only $6.50, plus mailing costs, as payment in full.

Print Name ....

Address ....

City & State .... Zip Code ....

☐ SAVE POSTAGE! Check here if you ENCLOSE $6.50 as payment in full—then WE PAY POSTAGE. Same return privileges with full refund GUARANTEED.

75360